Praise for *Secrets to Running a Lucrative Temp Desk*

'I couldn't recommend Sophie's book more. As an inexperienced recruitment consultant over ten years ago, I leant on Sophie's guidance and advice shared in this book to develop the traits of a high-performing consultant. Fast forward to my role now as a business owner and I ensure that all of my temp team members receive a copy of *Secrets to Running a Lucrative Temp Desk*. Their enthusiasm for the book is as strong as mine was as a consultant! With solid tips, tricks and strategies on how to gain loyalty from your temp staff to how to develop business development strategies so that your clients will never leave you, this book is jam-packed with information and I highly recommend it to anyone working on a temporary desk!'

Sinead Connolly, Co-Founder and Director, Lotus People

'When reading books like this I like to fold the corner of any pages that have helpful tips that will benefit me and my team in the future. I stopped this process after a third of the way through once realising I would end up with a book with every other page corner turned! The most impressive factor since implementing Sophie's book into our business has been the speed at which new recruiters have been able to convert their training into real-world results. A fantastic, concise and knowledgeable book which I recommend being used by recruitment companies around the world. It adds value and most importantly gives confidence to anyone working within the temporary recruitment market, whether they are fresh to the industry or have years of experience.'

Rem Kingston, Director, Diamond and RemTech, United Kingdom

'I ended up buying a further two copies of Sophie's book to give to two new consultants in my team. It is being used as a great learning device, with the three of us reading certain chapters every few days and then sitting down collectively and discussing what we learnt and what we can implement. New staff through to experienced directors can learn from this book. I cannot recommend it highly enough.'

Sebastian Leeder, Director, Construction, Gough Recruitment

'I found the book very inspirational, easy to read, understand and relate to. It felt like I was sitting in on a great training/seminar session! What a great read and so much to take on – so many logical steps and thinking about this industry. Sometimes you get so caught up in the everyday errands and administration of running a desk (among other underlying factors that keep you busy all day!) that you can forget to take a step back to think about the value-adding side of things … Or maybe we are never really taught to always have that as a priority in our business practices? Sophie's perspective is truly recruitment *consulting*. And I love it.'

Katerina Petrenko, Recruitment Coordinator, Rarekind: Recruitment and Human Resources Services

'Sophie Robertson's book *Secrets to Running a Lucrative Temp Desk* has been the staple diet of anyone who's commenced their career as a contract recruiter for Consultive. It's often referenced in placement celebrations, when solving a problem or when someone is crediting their learning on promotion. Thank you Sophie.'

Phil Isard, Founder of Consultive and Co-Founder of Amica Talent

'Sophie Robertson is quite simply the Queen of Temp. Sophie's *Secrets to Running a Lucrative Temp Desk* simply works. Across our teams it is common to hear the effects of Sophie's book and Sophie's training, such as 'eat the frog', 'multiple temp locations', 'specificity', 'Service, service, service and the money will follow'. Whether you're a white-collar desk, a tech desk or a blue-collar desk – if you follow her rules you cannot fail.'

James Purtell, Managing Director, Cox Purtell Staffing Services

'It is a truism that recruitment is simple but not easy. Sophie's book helps to cut through the clutter and make it that little bit easier. With relevant examples, easy-to-follow checklists and well-thought-out arguments, *Secrets to Running a Lucrative Temp Desk* is an awesome tool for both those new to recruitment and those who are old recruitment dinosaurs, like myself. The focus of the book is temp recruitment, but we use it as a training tool for contract and permanent recruitment as well, as many of Sophie's lessons are transferable across all types of recruitment. Sophie's book is part how-to guide, part motivational pep-talk and part manifesto for a better, more ethical recruitment industry. I genuinely think it is an essential read for any recruiter.'

Simon Moss, COO, The Recruitment Company

Sophie Robertson is widely regarded in Australia as the go-to expert on establishing, running and growing successful temp and contractor desks. Sophie started in recruitment in Sydney, Australia, in 1990 and in that time has set numerous records in relation to number of hours billed and profit made. In 2007, Sophie founded Younique Coaching, where she coaches recruiters and recruitment business owners to reach their potential and goals.

SECRETS

TO RUNNING A

LUCRATIVE

TEMP DESK

SOPHIE ROBERTSON

Interested in working with me?

If you would like to work with me to enhance your skills and grow your team, your business or your bottom line, you can do this in a number of ways:

- One-on-one coaching/mentoring
- Adding me as an advisor on your advisory board, or I can assist with establishing an advisory board for you, if you would like one
- Group training.

If you are unsure of what you need, the easiest thing to do is to get in touch for a no-obligation chat:

- + 61 448 173 307
- sophie@youniquecoaching.com.au
- App: Younique Coaching
- www.youniquecoaching.com.au

For my sons, Ruben and Fabian, who continue to be constant sources of inspiration, pride and joy.

First edition published in 2014.
This second edition published in December 2022.
© Sophie Robertson 2023
The moral rights of the author have been asserted.

NATIONAL
LIBRARY
OF AUSTRALIA
A catalogue record for this book is available from the National Library of Australia.

Printed book ISBN: 978-1-922611-58-1
Ebook ISBN: 978-1-922611-59-8

Cover art director: Natalie Winter
Cover design: Tess McCabe
Internal design: Production Works
Printed in Australia by Griffin Press

10 9 8 7 6 5 4 3 2 1

Disclaimer

Contents

Part two: For managers and recruitment business owners **135**

Introduction

This book is a how-to guide on running a best-practice temp desk, which in turn means a profitable desk that will ensure you build deep and long-lasting relationships with your temps and your clients. It might even be the most profitable desk in your space, as mine was when I was at Ecco Personnel, now known as Adecco.

This book is my way of documenting and passing on what I still consider to be best-practice temp service.

There is not only a need but a hunger for information on how to do the temp/contracting consulting job well. Too many people think temporary (temp) recruitment is the same as permanent (perm) recruitment, with the only difference being the placement's length of time. This couldn't be further from the truth. Perm consultants are matchmakers while temp consultants are employers of a mobile and remote workforce. The jobs are totally different, which is why they are suited to different people with different personality traits. Occasionally business owners will ask me, if a recruiter isn't particularly strong, whether they should put them in temp. On the contrary, to be a great temp recruiter you need to have a multitude of skills over and above what a perm recruiter needs.

If you are reading this I am heartened by the fact that you want to improve your skill level to increase not only your own professionalism but also the industry's overall. We can only expect and demand respect from the business community when we constantly strive to learn new skills and become adept at practising them. As Malcolm Gladwell – a journalist and bestselling author who frequently uses research from social science, sociology, psychology and social psychology – points out in his book about success, *Outliers*, mastery comes through hard work and practice: 10,000 hours of practice to be precise. This is where I got my recruitment stripes; when I add up my hours of experience over 18 years of converting prospects to clients and identifying and managing temps, the total number of hours easily doubles 10,000, and then some.

If you were in Australia in the early 1990s, you may remember the 'recession we had to have' according to the Honourable Paul Keating, our federal treasurer at the time. Can you imagine starting in recruitment when companies were laying people off by the hundreds? Well, that's what it was like. When I phoned clients, they would ask, 'Why are you calling me when I have to retrench 150 staff this week?' The number of people to be retrenched would vary, but otherwise the timbre of their responses was alarmingly similar.

Now when I look back, I am incredibly grateful that I started my recruitment career during tough economic times, because I quickly learnt what worked and what didn't. I learnt that three things rule in an economic downturn: persistence, relationship-building and temps.

Persistence rules because we know statistically that people need to have an average of four to seven touchpoints with us before they are ready to buy from us (except for referred clients).

Relationship-building rules because, unlike perm recruitment, people have to trust you to provide the right skill set before they give you a temp job order. Clients usually hire just one person to get a task done. For a permanent position, the client can interview several candidates and if the chosen candidate is lacking in certain skills, they can train them. Temps need to not only have the skill but preferably excel at it. The temp's task is to get the job done expertly and then exit – that is, unless they are offered a temp-to-perm position with the company, which is great for you as you earn both temp margins and a permanent placement fee. Plus it's a testament to your ability to find the right person with the right skill set and culture fit.

As we emerge from the global COVID-19 pandemic, where perm recruitment has been at the forefront due to skills shortages and potentially uncertain economic times looming, there has never been a better time to either set up your temp desk or improve how you run it to mitigate risk, and to bolster your earnings and improve the value of your recruitment business.

Temps rule because using temps is the perfect way for organisations to staff during uncertain economic times. They can use who they need, when they need, and only pay for the hours they use. Also, when times are tough, clients downsize and consolidate permanent staffing numbers. Often they cut too close to the bone and leave their remaining employees to battle on with extra work. The inevitable results are burnt-out employees, more sick days and less productivity. This is the perfect time to introduce temps into a company where the client pays for what they use and can finish up the temps at any time. What I saw in these situations was that the temp solution gave clients peace of mind in the short term and, over time, the temps would quietly and organically integrate into the company. In short, the clients came to rely extensively on the temps' contribution to the running of the company.

On the back of a solid temp desk, I was able to run the most profitable branch out of 30 branches nationally at Ecco. It was a desk I had built up from scratch in a relatively new office in Parramatta, during an Australian recession that made the Global Financial Crisis (GFC) of 2008 look like a small blip.

I eventually left Ecco after my maternity leave finished in 1997. When I returned to the workforce I joined a small boutique agency, Integrity Personnel, which incorporated other brands: Accountancy Search, Retail Staffing Solutions and a blue-collar division. I remember at the interview I asked how many temps they had out and was told 12 (approximately 384 weekly hours), to which I said, 'That's not a temp desk! If you want a temp desk, I can help you build and grow one'.

When I left after nine years of working on a part-time basis, the temp desk had, on average, 125 temps out, which equates to approximately 4000 hours per week. In chapter 14, I'll discuss why temps need to be measured in hours as well as headcount to grow a temp desk. Many recruiters only talk about how many temps they have out, but this doesn't give an accurate picture of growth or profit.

Okay, all that is history and what's it got to do with you? If you were working in recruitment during the GFC in 2007, you would know that many recruitment companies retrenched consultants and our industry noticeably shrunk. However, the companies with healthy temp desks not only survived but actually thrived. Unless you were in a niche recruitment company and/or had a temp desk, the GFC almost certainly played havoc with your billings if you were a consultant, or your business if you were a recruitment business owner. After some incredible years with a perm recruitment boom as a result of the global skills shortage exacerbated by the global pandemic, the economic outlook certainly looks a lot gloomier at the time of writing. We know that economies are cyclical and, while I hope you have been shoring up your client relationships and strengthening your temp processes these last few years, this book will assist you in building the temp arm of your recruitment business – which ensures a recurring income that will keep the lights on in your business when times get tough again.

Here are ten solid reasons you need to master running a temp desk:

1. It's recession-proof; in fact, challenging economic times are boom times for temps. While it's not too late to build a temp desk when times are tough, it's better to have the whole infrastructure set up and ready to roll. Otherwise the companies with established temp desks will steal the march on you because the clients already view them as trusted temp staffing providers.

2. According to IBISWorld, the recruitment industry is worth $50.4 billion annually in Australia with $34 billion of that being temp recruitment – so you want to ensure that you're getting a slice (or a bigger slice) of this considerable pie.

3. You never have to start the month with $0 on the board. If you only do perm recruitment, you can have the best month ever, but when the calendar clicks over to the first of the month, you're back to exactly $0 again – which can result in stress and even burnout.

4. Each temp consultant can consistently bill approximately $64,500 per month without having to rely on perms. This is based on having 1000 hours per week at an average margin of $15. If you think this is high and you don't think you can charge it, you will change your mind if you consistently implement the 'how-tos' in this book.

5. You will have better and more solid relationships with your clients. If your temps are part of the clients' key staff and you service the clients well, you will inevitably become a key factor in their business and success. Following my guide to best-practice temp service means you will be speaking with your temp clients on a weekly basis.

6. Clients will be more loyal to you. Your job is to make the clients look good in their companies. When staffing is done well and engagement is high, the clients get all the internal glory, which is how we want it.

7. You can become an industry expert very quickly and grow your desk almost without effort. Again, I will show you how in this book.

8. If you're a recruitment business owner, you add maximum value to your business by growing your temp desk, in case you ever want to sell up. There is a bonus chapter on this exit strategy and how to get maximum multiples for your business, written by mergers and acquisitions expert Rod Hore from HHMC (see chapter 19).

9. With more and more corporates hiring an increasing number of their permanent employees directly through their own talent acquisition teams, you are most likely losing perm revenue, so don't wait till it's too late. Lay the foundations for a solid temp desk and start earning part of the $34 billion in revenue on offer right now!

10. As a consultant, you can go on holidays and someone is working for you, so you don't lose income. When you do perm only, things can look very shaky when you go away and even affect your earnings when you return.

This book is written for novice and experienced recruiters as well as recruitment business owners. If you're a novice, good for you. You now get to learn the job as it needs to be done from the very start. No bad habits for you. You might like to refer to the glossary at the end of the book if you encounter any terms that are unfamiliar. If you're an experienced recruiter, you might be reminded of a few things you'd forgotten and maybe even learn some new tips and tools. After all, if you think you've got nothing left to learn, you will stagnate. As American leadership coach and management book author Marshall Goldsmith says, 'What got you here, won't get you there'.

If you're a recruitment business owner, you can use this book as a temp desk manual for training your staff and also as a GPS navigator for yourself, so you know what you need to keep an eye on.

While recruitment is not complicated, it is complex in that you need to understand what to do when and why. Once you've read this book and followed my blueprint for building the best temp desk on the planet, you will know when to do what, how to do it and what you need in order to do it. At the end of the book, I have provided a checklist of the things you need to do and think about to set up your best-practice temp desk.

When I use the word 'recruiter' in this book, I'm using it in the broadest sense to mean 'recruitment consultant' – that is, someone who attracts and enlists people and who gives advice on recruitment-related matters, which are very broad. For example, your advice may pertain to behavioural descriptive interview questions, psychometric tests, salary information, market intelligence, business wisdom and anything else relevant. Many people in the recruitment industry call themselves 'recruitment consultants' but do very little or no consulting at all. If you do not consult, which is to share your recruitment-related expertise, then there is no value to the client in using you. Algorithms can shortlist CVs and internal recruiters can interview. Their internal recruiter may not be as up-to-date on broad market salary advice, competitor and market intelligence, the latest sourcing strategies and so on. This all belongs in the 'consulting' part, so to be a good agency recruiter, you must recruit and consult to the client, and you must consult, advocate and work for your temps.

PART ONE

FOR CONSULTANTS

WORKING A

TEMP DESK

I've written this book in two parts. Part one is for consultants working a temp desk while part two is for business owners. That said, both parts contain essential information for anyone working in temp recruitment, so I encourage you to read them both!

Part one is the how-to. If you follow this part step-by-step, you will undoubtedly have success. This part of the book is a blueprint for success for you to follow. Our industry is mature enough that we do not have to make things up as we go. As the testimonials at the beginning of the book attest, many have triumphed in their careers and businesses by putting the learnings I've shared here into practice.

Chapter 1

The mindset of great consultants

Before I give you the complete toolkit on how to set up and run a profitable temp desk, you need to examine your mindset. Everything starts and ends with the mind. Without the right mindset, and without understanding the three key success factors I describe below, the toolkit is useless. This way you get to determine whether you even want to embark on this temp journey with me, or whether you're in the right career or hiring the right people to run your temp desk.

A consultant's mindset will determine the level of their success. As Stanford Professor of psychology Carol Dweck (whose primary research areas deal with motivation, personality and development) outlines in her book *Mindset: The New Psychology of Success*, successful people have a 'growth mindset' as opposed to a 'fixed mindset'.

Fixed-mindset people blame outer forces or circumstances for their lack of hours, sales or success. Have you heard recruiters blame the economy, or maybe even on occasion done it yourself? Even if the 'pie' of available business has shrunk, you have to consider where the remaining business is and how you can acquire it. Growth-mindset people ask questions as to how success can be achieved, rather than remaining passive victims of forces beyond their perceived control. A growth mindset means taking ownership of your skills and results, and realising that you can and must learn new skills.

I have seen examples of recruiters unaccustomed to having to search for and win business due to the niche they've been in. Some recruiters have had the luxury of being able to cherry-pick their jobs because they had no or very little competition. All I can say to them is, 'Wow, you have been fortunate. But as things have now changed and the market has moved, what do you need to know and do, not only to survive but to continue to thrive in your vertical?' Upon reflection, I know how fortunate I was to start in the recruitment industry during the recession: I learnt to make cold calls, dig out where the business was and convert prospects to clients. We also need to incorporate the advice from Malcolm Gladwell's book *Outliers* (which I mentioned in my introduction) that there are two main factors in mastery of your craft, which is what success is: opportunity – that is, the chance to practice your craft – and 10,000 hours of practice, a figure that emerged from all the case studies in his book.

So, the three key factors that lead someone to success are:

1. having a growth mindset
2. opportunity to practise their craft
3. 10,000 hours of practice.

As you are reading this book, you probably have a growth mindset already: you know you can improve your knowledge and skill level to set yourself up for success. If you are working as a recruiter, every day is an opportunity for you. What's important here is that you choose to do the activities that matter. As a recruiter, you have an endless number of seemingly conflicting priorities to deal with: do you do reference checks, check your inbox, call clients, call temps, do the weekly report for your boss, or something else? Your choice will determine how much 'practice' you get at doing the activities that matter and, therefore, how good a temp consultant you will become.

You must maintain focus and remember that great temp consultants do three critical tasks every day:

1. *Find quality temps:* source, attract, secure and retain great temps with the desired skill sets.

2. *Find quality jobs for their temps:* contact clients by phone, in person, via video call or via email (the latter being the least effective way to find job orders and temp vacancies).

3. *Match the right temps to the right clients:* regardless of whether that particular client has a job vacancy or not, if you know they use people with a particular hard-to-find skill, call the client if you have someone available and ask if they have that need now. For example, building material company Boral used to need cost accountants and, as they were rare, I'd always keep an eye out for them. Liquorland used to need accountants with Excel VLOOKUP skills; again, I was always on the lookout and would ask every accountant I interviewed to see how confident they were in this particular skill, and when I found one I'd phone Liquorland immediately. If you know it's a needle-in-a-haystack skill, don't wait till the client phones you and then start looking, or your chances of getting those hours becomes very low. Good temp consultants are proactive, not reactive.

Recruitment is a sales job

During my recruitment career, I've seen many good people leave this industry, and it's never been due to not knowing how to interview or recruit. It's always due to their lack of skills on the sales side. Some believed they weren't cut out for sales. This is what Professor Dweck would refer to as having a fixed mindset: we can always improve our skills and capabilities if we want to. Others have not known how to overcome their own aversion to selling and their self-image as a salesperson.

The good news about having a fixed mindset is that you can decide to change it to a growth mindset any time you want to by taking responsibility for your results and asking questions around how you can convert more sales.

If you have an aversion to sales, you first need be crystal clear that recruitment is a sales job. Think about it: you sell the job, the opportunity and the company to the temp, and you sell the temp to the company. By selling, I mean pointing out and emphasising the 'benefits' or 'what's in it for me' (WIIFM) – why it's good for the temp to take on this assignment or why this temp is right for this client. I don't mean manipulating the client or temp into doing something they don't want to do or that may be detrimental to them. The latter is how many people unconsciously think of sales and salespeople. Yet, when the discussion is lifted to the conscious level, most people can cite examples of how impressed they have been with a knowledgeable and caring salesperson who helped them out. You need to focus on defining what good sales service is and identifying with that type of salesperson, rather than the manipulative, sleazy one you may have in your mind and are therefore distancing yourself from.

The most important sale you will ever make is to yourself. How you view yourself informs your behaviour, which will ultimately determine your results and success. You need to come to terms with the fact that recruitment is a sales job, that a recruiter is a salesperson, and believe that you are providing real value to your clients. To not make contact with a prospect is potentially depriving someone of benefitting from your expertise. This is how I viewed it when I phoned a prospect; if I didn't phone them, they could be getting second-class service and not even know it. They should at least have the opportunity to say no to what I had to offer!

Even as a resourcer without business development responsibilities, your job is to make the jobs or your company sound attractive to your candidates and temps, which meets my definition of selling.

Once you are okay with being a salesperson in a sales environment, read on.

Chapter 2

Temp recruitment versus perm recruitment

The Australian recruitment industry is worth $50.4 billion per annum with 67% of this income coming from temps and contractors. The rest comes from perm recruitment and other types of recruitment fees.

The problems with hybrid desks

Most recruitment companies have a perm desk where perm recruitment is carried out for and on behalf of a client. Some of these companies will also have a temp desk, where a group of skilled temps and contractors are available for work and managed by one or more consultants.

The most profitable temp desks are run as specialist desks, *not* hybrid desks. Why? Because, as I mentioned in the introduction, perm recruiters are matchmakers. Their job is to make a match and hope the client and candidate live happily ever after. Temp recruiters are employers running a remote and mobile workforce. These are different jobs needing different skills.

Perm recruiters must understand what the client needs a prospective employee to do and who will be the best fit from a cultural and succession-planning point of view. The recruiter then makes a 'match' and gets paid a once-off fee for finding the best available person.

Temp recruiters have to do the same, while also making multiple matches for each new temp assignment, managing a remote workforce and ensuring that temps and clients are kept consistently happy by providing superior ongoing service.

For perm recruiters, the service ends once the person is placed (apart from the guarantee checks). For temp recruiters, the service begins in earnest when the temp is placed.

This means that, if recruiters run a hybrid desk, they will often be conflicted about what to do. There may be a client who needs second interviews organised for a permanent position where the placement fee is $25,000, and also a temp job available for a week which is going to net them $500 in temp margin. Many recruiters will choose to do the perm work first, which may mean that they lose the temp job – so that client isn't being serviced and a temp misses out on the work. It's a conflict that a consultant doesn't need to be subject to.

If you pay your consultants commission, they will usually work more on perm as the fees are instant while temp margins are a slower burn, but once you have built it up it will be ongoing and more reliable.

Which is best for profit?

Due to having to change speed and focus, having a hybrid desk is always detrimental to growing temp hours, which is detrimental to the agency's income. Temp income is like having money in the bank as long-term assignments just tick over and provide cashflow, certainty and solid profits.

Temps are often referred to as an agency's 'bread and butter' while the perms are the 'cream'. It's also said that the temp income is what keeps the lights on, as it's income that can be relied upon. You will get a better understanding of why this is when you read chapter 19, which focuses on valuation of a recruitment business for sale.

While a temp is working, you as the consultant earn a margin for every hour or day they work. Some temps/contractors are paid a day rate, in which case you earn a daily margin. If the temp is exceptional (which they will be once you implement the processes in this book) you will often earn a temp-to-perm placement fee as well. This is when the client offers the temp a permanent position with their company and it's accepted by the temp. Otherwise you get to place that temp with another client and the whole business of earning starts again! Does it get any better?

Specificity is key

For the purposes of simplicity, in this book I will refer to temps, casuals, on-hire staff and contractors as 'temps'. Please refer to the glossary at the back of this book for definitions of these and other relevant terms.

Temps are usually called in to perform a specific task or cover a specific position, so it's important to know exactly what they will be doing. The more information you can glean from the outset, the better equipped you will be to make the match. You need to be very *specific* in your communication, and ensure the client is as well.

Note that clients often use the terms temps, casuals and contractors interchangeably, so it's your job as a consultant to assist the client to define and specify what they mean and what they want.

A 'genuine' temp desk will have temps with documented skills ready to go when and where needed. It is not a genuine, professional temp desk if your client asks you for a temp and you need to scrounge around trying to find someone to see if they are interested in going to that assignment. Sure, if your temp desk is busy, fast-moving and growing, there may be a certain degree of scrounging, but that will be due to your increasing temp job orders – not due to your lack of planning. You must have temps set up and ready to go out to work at a moment's notice.

Skilled temps need to be thought of as an off-the-shelf 'product' that you can access any time. To do this you need to be proactive and constantly recruit for temps. You need to know what types of temps your clients need, and the type of temps you want to specialise in.

Chapter 3

How to set up a temp desk

To illustrate the process, let's say we're starting up a white-collar temp desk. These are the steps you need to follow.

1. Determine the categories of temps that you will be supplying

For our white-collar example we'll need:

- receptionists
- executive assistants (EAs)
- data entry operators
- contact centre operators
- customer service consultants
- accounts receivable officers
- accounts payable officers
- collections officers
- payroll officers
- accountants – financial, management and cost
- financial controllers.

2. Determine the skills needed for each category

Determining the skills needed will help you to take the right details for a temp job order and know what to ask when interviewing temps. Your job as a temp consultant is to ensure that your temps can confidently carry out the assignments you send them to. The temps have to feel comfortable and the clients need to receive value for money.

The skills and experience needed in our scenario include the following:

- *Receptionists:* type of switchboards used, number of lines and extensions, number of calls received per hour, number of visitors received per day, intercom usage for paging, typing, software skills, vocabulary and voice, personal presentation.
- *EAs:* Word, Excel, PowerPoint, Teams, Zoom, diarising, event organisation, screening phone calls.
- *Data entry operators:* fast and accurate alphabetical, numerical or alphanumerical data entry.
- *Contact centre operators:* inbound, outbound, order taking, returns, complaints, help desk, volume of incoming/outgoing calls, escalation process.
- *Customer service consultants:* as for contact centre operators.
- *Accounts receivable officers:* system/packages, number of debtors, amounts, days outstanding, invoicing, software.
- *Accounts payable officers:* system/packages, number of invoices, payment cycle, matching and batching, EFT, software.
- *Collections officers:* number of debtors, amounts chased, days outstanding, number of phone calls per day, escalation process.
- *Payroll officers:* frequency of payroll, number of pays, awards, enterprise agreements, payroll system.
- *Accountants:* financial, management, cost, system/packages, reporting, other duties (e.g. staff supervision and reports).
- *Financial controllers:* system/packages, staff reports, reporting deadlines.

3. Determine how you will test their skills

Some examples of tests might be:

- spelling tests
- basic numerical/mathematical tests
- typing tests
- data entry tests (numerical and alphanumerical)
- Word, Excel and PowerPoint tests.

Determine whether you want to test your prospective temps' skills in your office or whether you are happy for them to log in online and do the tests from home. The danger of them doing the tests from a place of their choice is that, theoretically, they could get someone else to do the tests for them, and you won't know until you send them to a job and the client tells you the temp doesn't have the skills required. Also, if they are allowed to do the test in their own time, they may not get around to it, which means you won't be able to use them. My recommendation is for them to do the testing while they are in your office for the interview – then they are ready to go to any assignment and you have peace of mind knowing that they can do what you told the client they could do. As mentioned earlier, it's critical that you know what the temp can do, as temps are needed to fill a particular gap with very specific skills.

4. Specify your benchmarks

Your benchmarks are the minimum standards that you will accept for a temp (determined by the test results). For example:

- spelling: 98% accuracy
- maths: 95% accuracy
- typing: minimum 60 words per minute with 98% accuracy
- data entry: alpha 8000 keystrokes per hour, numerical 10,000 keystrokes with 98% accuracy (some clients may say that speed is not important as long as the temp is accurate, but as a professional

temp consultant, your job is to provide temps who have both speed and accuracy)

· Word, Excel and PowerPoint: basic, intermediate and advanced (it's helpful here to have a copy of their test results, so you know exactly what they can do – e.g. they may be 'advanced' in Excel, but never had to do VLOOKUP).

Benchmarks are very important because they can be used to compare your temps' skills. If a client asks you why your temps cost $5 more per hour than another consultant's, you can ask what sorts of skills the cheaper temps have. More often than not, your competitor will not have advised the client or they may not even know themselves!

It's important that you do not get sucked into a discussion about price (the actual dollars and cents) with clients, but keep the discussion about value – value that you can demonstrate by showing that a faster and more accurate data entry operator will get the job done more quickly without the need for someone else to correct their work, which is in fact cheaper in the long run. The cheaper temp may require more hours to do the same job and require someone to both check and correct their work. When comparing temps, your client must ensure they are not only comparing apples with apples, but that they are actually comparing Red Delicious with Red Delicious. Otherwise it's like going to a Mercedes dealer and asking why their cars can't be had for the price of a Toyota. In the car example the point about value versus price is very obvious. So it is with temps. If the client wants to compare, you need to demonstrate your expertise by explaining the value gained by having higher-skilled and more accurate temps; that it would be completely fallacious to compare two people's skill levels without truly understanding what they are capable of. I'll talk more about this in chapter 7.

5. Recruit three to five temps in each category

Recruit three to five available people with the benchmarked skills for each job; for example, five clerks, five receptionists and five accountants. Remember that some people can belong in several categories; if you have an EA, the chance that they can answer a switchboard are quite high. The chance that they *want* to work on a switchboard, on the other hand, may not be as high, while some EAs will downright refuse to do switchboard work. We'll talk more about this in chapter 4.

6. Have a standard response time

Best-practice temp desks offer immediate service; I've always worked on a 20-minute call-back service, where the client has their booking confirmed within 20 minutes of calling a job order in. If I can't give them a confirmed name in that time, I'll still call them back within 20 minutes to let them know when I can fill the job by. Or, if I'm not confident I can fill the job, I'll ask them to go to another agency. The lead time till the job starts may simply be too short. Never take up all the available time trying to fill a job if you are unsure whether you can, or you've effectively made it impossible for any other agency to fill the job as well – which means you've left the client in the lurch. This is a no-no!

Remember that what you're selling when you sell temps is *peace of mind*. This means that your client does not have to fret about whether you're going to fill the job or when you might call back, which allows them to get on with their own job. The main advantage to you of filling your jobs in 20 minutes is that the client knows you will have the job booked, so they don't give the job out to other agencies. By acting effectively and efficiently, you fill more jobs, have more temps out working and bill more hours! The client is happy as they know you've taken care of the job and they can relax. The temp is happy as they know they have a job to go to. You and your boss are happy as you're growing your hours, desk and income.

In this example, we've focused on starting up a white-collar temp desk, but the process can be used to set up any type of temp desk: blue-collar, professional, retail, medical, hospitality, home care and so on. It's the same process, just different categories and skill sets. If you're setting up a blue-collar, retail or hospitality desk, you will need more people available in each category, these are traditionally high-volume temp desks. The number of available temps you require in each category will be governed by your clients' needs. The suggested three to five is to get a temp desk started from scratch, so you have some temps to market out and fill jobs with.

Chapter 4

How to recruit and manage great temps

As we have seen, recruiting for temps is vastly different to recruiting for perms. For perms, you want to know what the candidate's long-term career goals and aspirations are. For temps this is not really necessary information and can even distract you. However, it's still important to understand each person's motivations for seeking temp work, so you can do the best for them and your client.

Career versus short-term temps

In my experience I've found there are two types of temps:

1. People who really want a permanent job but are willing to temp in the meantime

2. People who choose to temp for their own reasons. They might be studying or travelling, only need to work part-time, want flexibility, not like working in the same place day in and day out, have religious reasons, want school holidays off, be writing a book, have a side hustle or have any number of other reasons. Sometimes these types of temps are referred to as professional temps or career temps.

If your client wants a long-term temp (six months or more) it's better to place someone who falls into category two and will be happy with this assignment rather than someone who really wants the security of a permanent job. That's because, if that candidate gets a permanent job offer, they will most likely exit your temp job, leaving you and your client in the lurch. It's up to you to prevent this from happening and to control as many variables as you can. Do the job properly the first time and you will save yourself lots of refilling and problem-solving later on.

You want to be the temp consultant who can anticipate problems and practise proactive prevention, as this is a sure-fire way to win! Understanding human nature and using empathy are vital skills for a top temp consultant. If you're concerned something might go wrong it most likely will, unless you take precautions.

Here's an example. Let's say your temp normally works for $38 per hour and you ask them to do a long-term assignment at $35 per hour. Chances are, at some point in that assignment they will pull out on you for a better-paying job. This is something you should anticipate. Rather than complaining about the temp's lack of loyalty, examine your own. If you truly understand their motivation for temping and what will keep them happy, work in their interest and they will repay you with loyalty, commitment and referrals.

If possible, aim to have at least 50% of your temp pool made up of career temps. It will make your life a lot easier. That is not to say that you don't want to have any candidates seeking permanent positions in your temp pool, but keep in mind that these temps will have a high turnover rate, which makes it harder to grow your hours by adding more temps. It may also affect the service you provide your clients, as you can't offer the same temps back to them. Some candidates seeking a permanent role are happy to work as a temp or contractor if they are kept in work. Challenges tend to arise if they are seeking a bank loan, though, as banks don't consider temp work to be as secure as a permanent job. It will be interesting to see how this shifts in alignment with the global trend towards the gig economy – where people choose to work in non-traditional ways – becoming a greater part of the workforce.

Where to find your temps

There are plenty of avenues you can investigate to find good temps:

- *Advertising:* online platforms such as Seek, LinkedIn, your agency website, university intranets, print media (although this is minimal now) and trade publications.
- *Word of mouth and referrals:* if you already have some temps out and you provide proper temp care, people temping for other agencies will seek you out for different reasons: more work available, better work with better companies, better pay rates, better temp benefits or better service. These are all factors that contribute to a temp deciding they want you to represent them. I recommend having a formal referral incentive program, although providing good service is usually the best incentive for people to refer you to other temps.
- *Conversation:* when you're out socially, ask people what they do.
- *Headhunting:* if you have heard about a particularly good temp, you can ask if they are happy with their current agency. Temps are like perm candidates: they can choose who they want to work for and when. Just like any employer, if a temp agency does not look after their temps, they will move.
- *Social media:* LinkedIn, Facebook, Twitter and so on.
- *Trade fairs:* exhibitions for specific trades or groups, e.g. for the electronics industry, Australian Defence Force or university students.
- *Pop-up booths in shopping centres:* I once set up a booth in a Westfield shopping centre at lunchtime and handed out flyers encouraging people to register if they were looking to change their jobs or they were unemployed. I even convinced a store manager to change industries and switch to working in recruitment.

- *Agency open days.*
- *Networking events:* most industries have their own events, e.g. the credit industry gathers at Australian Institute of Credit Management events; doctors go to medical professional development conferences. Find out where the people you want to attract go, and make sure you are there too.

Looking after your temps

Treat your temps well; value and appreciate them, as they are your employees. The fact that they turn up every day to your client's business makes them your best or worst ambassadors. It's up to you to look after them. If you don't know how, think about what you want from your boss. After having asked this question in many workshops, I know the answers are:

- recognition
- feeling valued
- appreciation
- being rewarded
- being part of the team
- being in the loop.

What are you doing to deliver the above benefits to your temps?

Always treat your temps with the same dignity and respect you would like to receive. Temp loyalty is earned by showing you care about them and their individual preferences.

Always be ethical; if a temp working for another agency wants to transfer onto your payroll and work for your agency, ensure it's done correctly so it is clear the temp instigated the transfer, not you.

Chapter 5

The essence of the temp interview

In the previous chapter we talked about treating your temps well so you can retain their services for you and your clients. But how do you identify and recruit the good – and great – temps?

What, when and how far?

There are three critical questions to ask when you interview temps:

1. *What will you do?* Notice this is different to 'what can you do?' Just because they can answer a switchboard doesn't mean they want to in a temp assignment. Remember your job is to keep your temps happy so they will be good ambassadors for you and keep your clients happy.

2. *When can you start, and for how long?* This means exactly when, so not 'ASAP' but 'tomorrow morning, and I'm happy to commit to a maximum of three months at a time'.

3. *How far will you go?* This relates to travel and, again, it needs to be very specific – not 'half an hour's drive', because that can mean different distances depending on where they drive from and the

time they start their journey. I discuss and get commitment on specific suburbs and locations each of my temps will travel to. I also find out how they will get there.

Since I only have 20 minutes to fill a job, I don't have time to ask each temp if they will go to a location, do the type of work required or whether they will commit to the timeframe. I need to know their answers to all those questions before I pick up the phone to book them in.

When I book in jobs for my temps, I tend to *tell* them I've booked them for work, rather than *asking* them. It sounds like this: 'Hi Susie, I've got a great job for you starting tomorrow for two weeks, doing exactly what you've been used to, and it's in the suburb next to home'. Then I give them the details and confirm them. It's an assumptive approach, but you can use it if you've done the work of asking the 'what', 'where' and 'how long' questions at the interview. I don't say, 'I'm calling to see if you're interested in doing this job'. There is simply no reason for them not to take the assignment, unless they aren't committed.

Sometimes you can't quite match all of someone's criteria. Then you can say something like, 'I know you said you didn't want to work in the city, but it's only for two days, and if you do this for me you will be first choice for any jobs close to your home. I need to call in a favour'. Most temps will do the odd assignment if you acknowledge it isn't their preferred job (so they know you listened and care) and you have a good relationship with them. If you can't get your temps to do your assignments, you're either not being firm enough or they don't respect you or feel heard.

The best temps are flexible, reliable and have common sense. Some people have great skills but have difficulty settling into an unfamiliar environment and therefore will not do their best work.

Define the temp's skills

Further to the 'what will you do' question, you need to determine (and then test) the skills that the temp is prepared to use on an assignment.

Have a tick sheet with very specific skills they can select. For example, say 'Ericsson switchboard' rather than just 'switchboard', and specify alphabetical or numerical data entry rather than just data entry. Just because they've used one switchboard doesn't mean they won't need training to use another. It's vital for you to be able to tell your clients exactly the skills the temp has and what training they will need, if any.

Having happy clients is partly about managing expectations. For example, if you tell a client that your temp has previously used an Ericsson switchboard with 10 incoming lines and 200 extensions for 12 months, they will expect them to be proficient with it, whereas their expectations will be very different if the temp only did relief reception work one day a week using that switchboard.

You need to know specifically what the temp can do so that you can pass that knowledge on to your client. Likewise, you need to know specifically what the client wants the temp to do in the assignment so the temp knows what to expect. This is the area of expertise that defines your competence as a temp consultant: the ability to take a thorough and accurate job order and find the closest match in skills that you can. If you are not really *specific* about the information required, the probability of getting it wrong is high, with the end result that you lose credibility and trust with both client and temp.

You also need to ensure that the temp has a valid working visa if they are not a citizen or permanent resident. For some niches, such as blue-collar manufacturing clients, they may also need relevant tickets to perform the work, such as a forklift licence.

Lastly, can you find out a 'fun fact' about your temp – something about what their hobbies are or what makes them different? This shows that you are interested in them and also better able to describe them to clients as a three-dimensional person rather than just a two-dimensional recital of their CV. People hire people, so make sure you know your temp as a person as well. For example, do they like hiking, ice skating, Scandinavian crime novels or cooking?

Specificity is gold

I am obsessed with some things, and one of them I express by saying, 'specificity is gold'. Anyone I have coached, trained or mentored knows that this is one of my mantras.

Cast your mind back to a situation of conflict with either a client or temp, or even in a personal relationship. Consider whether the conflict arose because someone wasn't specific enough in their communication. Usually this is the case.

It may have been that you assumed the client had read and agreed to your terms of business but, because you neglected to talk to them and get their express agreement and signature, there is now a conflict after you have found them the temp (or, worse, after the temp has already done the job and needs to be paid!). Or it may be that you asked the temp to call you if they couldn't go to an assignment, but you didn't specify when they had to call you, so they called your client in the morning and only phoned you in the afternoon after missing a whole day of work.

There are countless examples, and I'm sure you have some of your own. The way to master the temp consulting job is to reflect when something goes wrong: 'What could I be more *specific* about next time to avoid a similar situation?'

By being really specific, you get rid of assumptions and have a real chance of preventing a problem before it even arises. Look at your potential conflict situations and prevent them from recurring by instilling some 'rules'.

Rules matter

Have you ever played a game of Monopoly and, at some point in the game, disagreed over the rules with other players? This can easily be avoided if you set out the rules from the beginning and get agreement from all players. It's exactly the same with temp and client relationships. Being in control is part of displaying your expertise and professionalism. If you know what to do but skip the steps, quite frankly you deserve the problems you encounter later on.

The next step of the interview is to explain how you need your temps to work with you in order to deliver as many assignments as possible for them, and to gain their agreement to your 'rules'. In my experience in sales and in life, people will agree to do what you ask if you tell them what benefits they will get out of it. In other words: what's in it for them.

This is what I would say:

> 'We work on a 20-minute call-back service, which means that we call our clients back within 20 minutes of them giving us a job, giving them the name of the temp booked for the assignment regardless of whether the job is to start tomorrow or in three weeks' time. What I need to know from you is whether I can book you in without speaking to you in case I can't get hold of you? I know what you will do and where you'll go, so all I need is your availability. You need to tell me if your availability changes, as 20 minutes goes by very quickly, and if I have to call five temps to ask if they are available, I'll use up all my time and not be able to give the clients top-level service. The happier our clients are, the more jobs we have, which means that I can keep you in work. It's okay if your availability changes, but you must let me know immediately and not when I have a job for you. If I know you're not available, I just won't call you. Better for both of us.'

I'd then go on to explain:

> 'If you haven't heard from me and I know you're available, it's helpful if you can call or text me around 3 pm to see if there are any new jobs that are suited to you. This also keeps you at the forefront of everyone's minds and we know you're keen to work with us. Does this sound okay? Let's start today so you can get into the habit.'

This part of the interview process is critical and must not be skipped. Doing this well will save you time and effort at a later date. It's about temp control and setting the parameters of the relationship. If you don't tell them the 'rules', they will make up their own. It's also a great litmus test to see if they call you the first day you ask them to. If they do, they have every potential to become a great temp. If they don't, this should act as a warning bell; explain the process to them again, get their commitment again and test them again.

Another rule to set applies to when they are actually on assignment. Tell them that you want to ensure their happiness in a job and therefore would like to speak to them weekly while they're on the assignment. Jobs change and sometimes they may get asked to perform additional duties, which may warrant a pay rise. Or sometimes the workload may increase and they may want to avail themselves of the overtime option, which you can help facilitate for them. Tell them it's best if they call you when they have a spare couple of minutes as you may call them at a busy time. Again, get agreement from them that they will do this. If you do not speak with your temps weekly, it is just the same as coming to work every day and having your boss ignore you. How would you like that?

Your agency may also have rules around mobile phone and internet usage while at work – for instance, only accessing the internet for work purposes or checking their phone during their lunch break.

Now you need to tell the temp about how you pay and what they need to do to get paid. I advise using the same words at every temp interview, so you know exactly what you've said and you have a consistent interview process.

If your week goes from Monday to Friday, you might want them to email you their time sheet by 5 pm on Friday. Advise them on when their pay will be in their account. Depending on which award you pay them under, pay day might be the following Tuesday or another day. It's their responsibility to give you their correct bank details and tax file number so they can be taxed appropriately. Tell them to call you if their manager isn't around to verify their time sheet so you can chase up a signature for them. It's very important that you pay your temps on time, to keep them happy, but also so you can invoice your client. You can't count the hours as billed if you haven't invoiced them!

Temp availability list

Once the temp has left the interview, you must put all the information you have gathered on an availability list. How good this list is will to a large extent determine how quickly you can grow your hours: a comprehensive and specific list means that the temps will actually agree to the assignments when you contact them.

The availability list needs to have on it the following information:

- *Name:* the name that they prefer to be called (for example, Sandra Citizen may rather be called Sandie).
- *Phone number:* their number and an alternative, such as their partner's or dad's.
- *Location:* where they live, so you can assess travel time. Also include where they are willing to travel to.
- *Skills:* details of their experience and the results they have achieved in your tests.
- *Transport:* do they have their own car or do they need to work close to public transport?
- *Start date:* if they say they are available ASAP, ask if that means tomorrow. Sometimes they'll say, 'Oh no, not that soon', so be specific and nail it down to a date.
- *How long they are available:* the maximum length assignment they are willing to take.

I cannot stress enough how important it is to have this list, and to make sure the information on it is accurate and up-to-date. Without this, it's impossible for you to fill a job quickly and efficiently. If you offer a 24-hour service, you need to have this list with you all the time, whether in hard copy or in an easily searchable electronic format. Hopefully you have this availability on your CRM, so you don't have to double up and have information on separate spreadsheets.

Verbal reference checks

Finally, you must do verbal reference checks with a prospective temp's referees. In my career, I have seen some fraudulent written references that were only unearthed when we phoned to do the verbal reference checks. One referee said they had never given that person the written reference that we had a copy of! It turned out the applicant had stolen the company's letterhead before leaving and was forging the manager's signature.

Through verbal reference checks you can confirm specific details about someone's flexibility and common sense, which are critical traits in a good temp. Make sure you do your due diligence on the referee. If you are given a name and a mobile number, you actually don't know who you are speaking to. A recruiter even admitted to me that he had posed as a referee for five of his friends! Your due diligence may be to:

- Call the company the referee works for on a landline, if they have one.

- Do a video call so you can compare their likeness to their online photos, say on LinkedIn.

- Ask them to send you an email from their business email to confirm their position in the company.

- If it's an email reference, check the IP address they respond from.

There are companies that will do reference checking for you, which is time saving but may rob you of hearing first-hand about the temp's strengths that you can use as selling points to clients. Of course, reference checks are excellent ways to market to the referee as well.

Here are some questions that you need to ask in a verbal reference check:

- Did Joe show common sense? Can you give me an example of when Joe demonstrated common sense in his job?

- Would you describe Joe as a flexible employee? Can you give an example of this flexibility?

- How does Joe perform when thrown into a new environment/ team? What type of new situation has he been thrust into while working for you?

- Was Joe reliable and punctual?

- Would you recommend Joe to a future employer?

- Would you rehire Joe?

- Are you the person who hires temp staff for your company?

- (If the answer to the above question is yes) As Joe is available for work right now, what do you have that I can book him for?

Ask the potential temp about the referees they have put down. You will need at least two referees to call and they need to be people the temp reported to, preferably in temp jobs and/or their most recent jobs. If the former, this will also immediately provide you with potential sales leads as you know the referees use temps. Take the opportunity to ask who hires temps in their company and offer the temp that you are reference-checking straight back to them. These are the quickest and easiest temp jobs you're ever going to uncover.

Walking dollar temps

If you've been in recruitment before, you will recognise a 'walking dollar temp' when you see one. They are the temps you can send anywhere and know they will impress your clients. Temps are not like a shelf product that you can store until you sell them. If you don't keep your temps in work, they will work elsewhere, and then you've lost them. This is true for any good temp, but for a walking dollar temp, their shelf life is almost non-existent. I market these temps straight away, preferably while they are still in my office. How impressed would they be if you got them a job before they left the interview? Call ten of your clients and market that temp to them. In my experience, when I did this, I would get at least two jobs within 24 hours. You can also ask your temp to nominate five to ten companies they would love to work for. Call those companies while the temp is in front of you. The loyalty you get from them by displaying that you're actually working proactively to get them a job cannot be underestimated. Even if you don't manage to secure them an assignment before they leave your office, they will work within with your rules as they can see you are genuinely trying to secure them a job.

If you can't get your walking dollar temp a job before they leave your office, promise them that you will pull out all stops to place them. You can ask them in return not to take another assignment as you will be marketing them heavily. To be fair to them, give them a deadline such as 36 or 48 hours, which will also provide you with the urgency to hunt out that job order for them. Your pay-off will be the strong likelihood of the assignment being extended or even going perm, as your client will also recognise the quality of the temp.

Here are some characteristics of a walking dollar temp so you can identify them when you encounter them:

- well groomed
- excellent skills
- friendly
- adaptable
- flexible
- reliable
- intelligent
- common sense in spades.

Chapter 6

How to sell temps

Now you've got all those short-shelf-life temps on your books, you must get some job orders, or you'll lose the temps – and then when you do get job orders, you won't be able to provide a quick and efficient temp service.

A recruitment consultant is like a juggler who is constantly juggling three balls: these are the three critical tasks of a successful consultant that I introduced in chapter 1. These are the three balls:

1. *Finding quality temps:* sourcing, attracting, securing and retaining great temps with the desired skill sets.
2. *Finding quality jobs for your temps:* contacting clients by phone, in person, via video or via email.
3. *Matching (reactively and proactively) the right temps to the right clients:* regardless of whether that particular client has a job vacancy or not, offering the client someone who you know would suit their business, especially if their skill set is hard to find.

Just like a juggler, you must keep all three balls in the air at once. If you only concentrate on getting more temps without calling clients to find jobs, you will lose the majority of your temps as their shelf life is extremely short. Most temps can't afford to sit around and wait for you to find them jobs. If, on the other hand, you only do business development without replenishing your temp pool, you won't have any temps to fill the jobs when you get them. Therefore, you need to dedicate time to all three of these critical tasks.

The very best recruiters do these three tasks every day. They don't get sidetracked by other things. And, let's face it, there really are a lot of tasks on a temp desk that are peripheral to the main game: answering emails, returning phone calls, doing reference checks, sourcing and posting on LinkedIn and other places. While these tasks are necessary, they are not critical. By critical, I mean if these tasks are not completed you will either fail at being a good temp consultant or you will have huge peaks and troughs in your hours and billings. These peaks and troughs are commonly referred to in the industry as champagne and razor blades: champagne when you have a great month and razor blades when you have nothing on the board and nothing in the pipeline. The latter is obviously not the best way of building your career or income stream. Also, some recruitment companies may not be willing to 'carry' you if you have too many razor-blade months. So, for your own peace of mind, earning capacity, reputation, professional growth and work security, make sure you do your three critical tasks every day. Yes, there will be days when you might be putting out fires and you don't have a whole lot of time to make those business development calls, but even if you only manage four sales calls, that's better than none. It's a matter of establishing a habit that will guarantee your success.

Where to look for temp job orders

The first place to look for new temp job orders is your current temp and perm clients. We know it's a lot easier to sell to an existing client than to a brand-new client. A new client also takes time to convert, particularly in the case of temps, as it's more of a risk for the client. With permanent positions, the client can compare your candidates to another agency's by interviewing them for the same job. This enables them to compare not only the quality and suitability of the candidates but also your service level. For temps, only one agency gets to fill a job, so when they 'try' you, they are taking a risk. My experience is that you need an average of five or six touchpoints (contacts) with a client to build up enough trust for them to give you a temp job. The bigger the usage (the dollar spend of the account), the longer it takes to convert them. Most key accounts have taken me six to nine months to convert. But when they do convert, you suddenly have lots of hours with very healthy margins due to the sheer volume of work these accounts can provide.

When you take a permanent job order, ask if the client needs a temp in the meantime, so they don't have to rush to hire someone in a certain timeframe. Always ask the client if they want the best person available for a job rather than the first available person. In reality, for a permanent position most clients want to hire someone who is already in the workforce, which means the candidate will have a notice period that needs to be honoured before they can start with the client company. Yet, some companies will still attempt to hire a replacement person to cross-train with the outgoing person. A better solution would be for you to offer a temp who can be cross-trained by the incumbent person and who can fill in until the permanent replacement is identified, and then train the new employee. This gives the client a better chance of securing the best person.

Remember that, as a 'consultant', your job is to consult, which means giving clients sound business advice that will serve them in the long run. You will find that being a trusted advisor is an excellent basis for building a business partnership, rather than being the transactional recruiter who is only there to put someone into a position. Clients do not value transactional recruiters, and it is increasingly difficult for them to justify their fees. Consider that your clients are paying for your expertise in all matters recruitment – not just your ability to fill a job order.

Also, ask if temp-to-perm is an option. Usually your temp will have a better chance of getting the permanent job because they get to display what they can do on the job. Even if you don't get the temp-to-perm placement, you are still more likely to get your candidates interviewed as you will be in more frequent contact with the client than other agencies, if you adopt my suggested best-practice service to clients as outlined in chapter 10.

Your client's competitors can be another great source of new temp job orders. Say you already have one telco on your books. It is very easy to call other telcos to offer your services as you already have knowledge of their industry and, more than likely, temps with telco experience and skills. This is also an excellent way to build your personal brand if you're working for a generalist agency. As I dealt with the two largest electronics companies in Australia, I started attracting people with electronics experience, which then made it a lot easier for me to market to other electronics companies. Inadvertently I became the 'go-to' electronics consultant for clients, temps and candidates.

Your competitor's clients are another source. As mentioned earlier, reference checks can help you discover if companies use temps. Your best source of information is the people you interview. Ask where they've worked, who you can call for reference checks and whether it was a good place to work. Just like with perms, it's far preferable for you to place your temps with reputable companies boasting good working conditions.

Case study: Merck Sharp & Dohme

When I started in recruitment in 1990, I had to make 30 calls a day and call every client on a fortnightly roster. One of the companies I called was Merck Sharp & Dohme (MSD), one of the four largest pharmaceutical companies in the world at the time. The reason I called them was that the market was very tight, with 11.5% unemployment and many redundancies. I had to go where I knew there was temp business. At MSD, an American-owned company, they had many temps on site and they'd had the same on-site agency supplying them for roughly ten years.

I called the HR coordinator, who was always polite and professional towards me; we'd have a pleasant chat but, essentially, I wasn't getting anywhere. I couldn't get to speak to one of the HR managers, I didn't get any job orders and there was no real prospect for me to get any business despite phoning every single fortnight for about seven months. What was I to do?

One late Friday night in the office after everyone else had left, I pondered whether it was time I stopped calling MSD and replaced them with another company where I might actually be able to convert the client. Yet, it seemed such a waste to stop after so much consistent effort. I looked up the *Who's Who*, which was an annually updated print reference book that listed all the important people in a company. I looked up the name of the Managing Director for MSD in Australia and called him. It was 6.30 pm on a Friday night. Much to my surprise, when I asked for the MD by name, I was put straight through to him! It was so easy, yet also terrifying as I was still a relatively new consultant. We had a chat and he asked me nicely but directly, 'What is it you want?' An excellent question, to which I answered, 'Well, I was wondering how you know you're still getting the best people and the best service at the best price when you haven't used any other agency for ten years?' There was a pause and he said, 'You have a point, but you know I have people who look after HR for me. Can you call on Monday and speak to one of the HR managers?' He gave me the person's name.

I was absolutely over the moon. After seven months of getting nowhere, I thought I might finally be on my way. I called bright and early the following Monday morning and, before I had finished introducing myself, the HR manager said, 'Oh, you're the one who called our MD on Friday night... what were you thinking?' We chatted for a while and then he asked what I wanted. I replied that I wanted a 20-minute meeting to discuss his temp staffing needs.

As I was leaving his office after the visit we passed by the HR coordinator, who he asked to give me the next job order so they could try us out! It was so exciting; the fact that it took another four weeks to actually get the job and that the job was apparently a 'difficult' one did not deter me at all. It was the beginning of a mutually fruitful business relationship.

Here are the lessons I learnt from calling MSD:

- *When you're marketing, always go straight to the top.* It doesn't matter if the person you call doesn't do the actual recruitment. If they say 'call Joe Blow', then Joe Blow will take your call and listen to what you have to say because you've spoken to his boss (or even his boss's boss, as in my case!). This can save you a lot of time in the long run. It might save you seven months of your life – the time it took me to learn this lesson.

- *Call out of hours.* This is the best tactic if you want to get hold of high-level people, as the receptionists and EAs will have gone home. Interestingly, the person who put me through to the MD was the actual gatekeeper – the person who raises the boom gate to their site. That was his job. His job wasn't to screen phone calls like the people we normally understand to be 'gatekeepers' – that is, receptionists and EAs. Today you can often reach high-level people more easily via their mobile numbers, as these are often displayed on websites and LinkedIn.

People in high-level positions are, on the whole, professional and unlikely to be rude or hang up on you. After all, I don't think one gets to MD level at MSD without being professional. This means that you will get a more considered response to your calls, if not necessarily a warmer one.

Marketing temp services

What is the best way to sell temps, or any other recruitment service for that matter? Some ways are to ask for referrals from existing clients, blogging to showcase your expertise, tendering proposals, or simply making contact with a company to ask how they go about recruiting for temps. When you're starting out and building your hours, you really need to be making contact with potential clients or prospects. Some recruiters and recruitment trainers say you shouldn't be calling potential clients to market your services as they consider cold calling a demeaning way to acquire new business, but I'm of the opinion that, if there's someone you'd love to deal with, the quickest way of establishing contact with that company is to make the contact yourself. Of course, you need to make the call interesting and, therefore, warmer for them; you have to engage them from the beginning. I'll cover how to do just that in this chapter.

Statistically we know it takes on average between four and seven direct contacts (touchpoints) before someone will buy from us, unless they are a referral. As I mentioned earlier in this chapter, in my experience in the recruitment industry I've found it actually seems to take an average of five to six contacts. That doesn't mean that I haven't gotten a job order on the first phone call at times: I have. But I put that down to good timing more than anything else. (Sometimes I knew they had a vacancy before I made the call.) It also doesn't mean that it hasn't taken me a lot more touchpoints to crack some major accounts. The biggest accounts took me six to nine months to crack. What made them major accounts was the fact that they already used lots of temps from a well-established competitor agency. As I mentioned earlier, when you want to persuade a company to switch from a tried and tested agency to you, it's a big risk in their eyes, and therefore it takes time to build enough trust.

Thinking about the average number of touchpoints before we convert a temp client, the flow from start to finish might look like this:

1. Introductory call
2. Handwritten card with business card attached to follow up initial phone call. (Snail mail? Yes! People love it and it will make you stand out even more during these digital times. After all, don't you love getting handwritten mail?)
3. Another phone call/email

4. Client visit using a consultative sales approach and asking for the business
5. Follow-up phone call
6. Email/phone call/SMS.

Each touchpoint is about building trust, finding out about your prospect's needs and challenges, and displaying your expertise and professionalism until the client feels comfortable enough to give you an opportunity. When that opportunity comes, you must be ready with excellent temps available and must service your client efficiently and effectively.

Important points to remember before you pick up the phone

When calling companies to offer your services, there are a number of important things to remember:

- It's never about you when you're selling, but always about your client. So, do not start with a sales pitch where you ramble on about who you are and what you do. The client simply doesn't care. Theodore Roosevelt said, 'No-one cares how much you know, until they know how much you care'.

- Some people say you should never cold call, so let me be clear on my definition of a cold call. A cold call is simply the first time I speak to a client. For example, I may have been dealing with a company for a while and a new hiring manager starts. The first time I call that person is a cold call for me even though I know the company very well. I may get a referral to someone, and even though there is a reason for the call, it's still the first time I speak to that particular person, so I define it as a cold call. It's impossible to build a desk and grow your hours if you only speak to people you already know!

- While it may be the first time you speak to someone, you can still emphasise whatever connection there is to make the call warmer and more interesting for the other person. In my experience you have the initial ten seconds to grab their attention: this seems to be the timeframe in which the client will decide whether or not they want to engage in conversation with you. My opening line is often something like this: 'I'm calling you for two reasons. One reason is that I deal with your major competitor and, in the process of interviewing for them, candidates have enquired about your company. The other reason is I noticed you just launched an exciting new product'. Naturally you have to think of two reasons that are relevant to their company, but the power in this opening is that it's *all* about them, and you don't sound like you're calling them as one of 30 companies on your call list for the day. This is a way of making them feel special.

- Have purpose: why are you calling? If you don't know or you're doing it for the sake of meeting your KPIs, the prospect will be able to tell that you're underprepared and that you're there for you and not them. Also, as the call is your initiative, you need to be steering the agenda. Don't ramble on, as this shows a lack of respect for the prospect's time as well as your own.

- Devise a wish list. When you were little, did you write a wish list for Santa? Did you have your list in descending order of the size or dollar value of the wish? If so, you know exactly what I mean! You need to have a list of desired outcomes for each call (and visit, for that matter).

- The question to ask yourself is this: if you could have anything you want from a client marketing call, what would it be? And if you can't get the biggest wish, what's your next wish?

My wish list always had five things on it:

1. Job order
2. Client visit

3. Referrals to other hiring contacts

4. More information about their hiring intentions, what else they have planned, etc.

5. For them to say 'thank you' to me for calling them.

My old boss taught me that last one. Once this came onto my wish list, the quality of my calls changed, as the only way I could get someone to appreciate me calling them was to give them 'value' on the call. Value meant I had to become an expert in their company, industry and the economy so I could not only hold a business conversation but also, with any luck, tell them something they didn't already know. One time a client said to me, 'The only time I find out anything about what's going on in our company is when you call'! In the age of Google alerts, it's so incredibly easy to be notified of news on any topics, keywords or company names that you want to know about. Whenever Google finds a new article containing the keywords, you get an email alert with a link. There is simply no excuse for not being commercially aware now.

Some helpful conversation starters and useful questions

Since it's all about your client, you need to be enquiring with a curious mind when you make the initial call. Use open-ended questions that start with 'how', 'what', 'when' and 'who', but use 'why' cautiously because it can be misconstrued as you questioning their right to choose. A softer and more effective way of asking 'why' is, 'May I ask what the reasons are that you choose to do it that way?' Open-ended questions can't be answered with a 'yes' or 'no', so they are useful for engaging the prospect and fact-finding about the prospect's challenges and buying preferences. Closed questions will quickly cut off any real chance of a conversation. If you ask 'Do you use temps?' and they say 'no', the door is closed, and while you can prise it open again, it's better not to slam it shut in the first place.

Here are some useful open-ended questions for new calls:

- 'Are you the right person to speak to regarding the hiring of…?' (This one is closed as you do not want to waste your time speaking to someone who does not have any decision-making power.)
- 'How do you generally go about it?'
- 'How do you normally cover for holiday and sick leave? What about extended leave, e.g. parental leave or long-service leave?'
- (If they use agencies) 'How do you decide which agency to use?'
- 'How do you find the temps and the service that the agency offers?'
- 'What do you like about your current providers?'
- 'What have you disliked about their service?'
- 'Are there any other decision-makers besides yourself?'
- 'Who else might benefit from my service?'
- 'When is a good time for us to meet?'

Notice how the aim here is to get them to talk, show interest in them and also gain information about what they look for, so you can market your features and benefits appropriately.

Closed questions are also useful when you are ready to 'close', which means to get agreement or commitment to something. For example:

- 'If you have a permanent vacancy, would you use a temp during the hiring process to give yourself plenty of time to find the right candidate?' We want to 'close' on them agreeing to use a temp and possibly extend the time to find a permanent employee, if required.
- 'Next time you need a temp, do you feel comfortable enough with me and our company to give that job to us?' This is a trial close before you then ask for the job.

Case study: LG Electronics

The first time I called LG Electronics, it had rebranded from Goldstar to LG and was really exploding onto the Australian market. When

I introduced myself, the HR manager sighed and asked me, 'You're a recruiter and you want to know how we recruit, right?' It was clear that she had taken many calls from other recruiters trying to elicit business! Essentially, yes, I did want to know how they recruited, but I knew I had to present a good reason for her to want to continue that conversation with me. You have to empathise with HR or talent acquisition (TA) people who often have to take scores of phone calls from recruiters who are just in it for a quick transaction and fee. Also, many unskilled recruiters will focus on themselves and how great they are, which is a complete anathema to clients.

This is what I said to her: 'Actually, I'm calling you for two reasons. Firstly, I deal with your major competitor and in the process of interviewing for them, candidates have asked me about your company as well. Secondly, I've noticed all the sexy advertising you've been doing lately on TV'. This basically opened up the conversation as there was something in it for her to speak with me about: potential experienced electronics staff. Plus, I find that clients are always interested in speaking with you if you deal with their competitors. It may be just out of curiosity, or there could be an element of FOMO (fear of missing out).

The comment about their TV advertising was more about paying them a compliment and showing that their marketing efforts were working. Clients are always interested in feedback about the perception of their brand in the marketplace. Similarly, humour can be a good tactic: if you can make someone laugh, then you've managed to create instant rapport as laughing is involuntary.

What happened next I put down to timing: at the end of that conversation, I got three permanent job orders. I want to be clear that getting a job order on a first call is definitely a bonus, but it wasn't the real aim of my call. If you are into transactional recruitment where you get a job, place it and then move on, then that would be the reason for the call.

Recruitment has evolved so much over the three decades since I started out. At one point the transactional model was almost extinct, but the skills shortage exacerbated by the global pandemic made this form of recruitment possible again. Many companies have in recent years moved towards having internal TA teams, as online platforms have made it easier for them to source and recruit themselves. While these TA teams predominantly recruit for permanent positions, there has been an increase in them hiring their own casuals and contractors as well.

As recruiters, we must build relationships with clients and truly understand their businesses so we can proactively advise them on how they can recruit better-quality people while enhancing their brand in the employee market. The advantage of doing this is that the clients will regard you as the 'expert' and, in my experience, if you come up with the idea or solution, you will get to deliver it as well. It's unlikely that they will get one of your competitors to deliver a brainchild of yours.

In summary:

- Calling your clients' competitors is an easy way to create relevance when you phone.
- You might as well use the industry knowledge and temps you already have by making that industry your area of expertise.
- Be interested in the client, their job, their company and their challenges.
- Be interesting to the client you are phoning.
- If you're not able to be both interested and interesting, always choose to be interested as it's always about the client first.
- A compliment goes a long way, as does humour.

Case study: David Jones

Here is an example of defining a 'problem' the client didn't even know they had. I had been dealing with David Jones for a couple of Christmases supplying them with doormen. You may know these doormen who, for the month of December, open the door for you at flagship David Jones stores in their grey top hats and coats on a red carpet. When I enquired as to how they recruited the rest of their temps, I was surprised to find that each store used a multitude of agencies for temps on the dock and in store. Each store manager had their own way of recruiting. I contacted the procurement officer in charge of staff recruitment and suggested that I knew how the group could save money.

It's always important to understand the person you're dealing with and what their specific job is. In procurement the job is to source the best price, which is why I used that particular opening when I contacted them. HR's job is to source the best people, so if my call had been to HR, I would have focused more on how I could get them better-quality people across the board, so their culture would remain intact or be further enhanced.

I was also fortunate with my timing as David Jones had recently appointed a new CEO who had tasked procurement with re-examining the prices they were paying for various items. This edict led to them replacing the shopping-bag supplier they had dealt with for umpteen years, as they were no longer the most competitive in their pricing.

It was into this environment that I called procurement, which likely made them more receptive. A meeting was set up, and I went to speak with procurement and explained that, because they were using a multitude of agencies nationally, they couldn't control the quality of service and temps provided. And, more importantly, they weren't getting the advantage of using their considerable buying power. An example I use is this: if you go into a hotel and want a room for one night, you end up paying their 'rack rate'. However if you go into the hotel and say, 'I am after a deal for myself and 20 of my colleagues, who will use your hotel once a quarter', you will get a discount simply by combining your buying power. It becomes in the hotel's interest to give you a more attractive deal, or one of their competitors might and they'll miss out altogether.

Procurement asked me what I would suggest, and I said they should put out a tender and see what services and prices they might attract for supplying them with temps. The meeting ended with them saying they would consider my suggestion.

A few weeks later I received an invitation to tender for their temp services nationally. The good news was that I was invited to tender. The problem was that I was general manager for a boutique recruitment agency operating out of one office in Parramatta, clearly unable to provide temps nationally from a practical perspective.

I called procurement and asked if they would consider awarding the tender by state, as I was confident we could service New South Wales. They replied no, as they had found my arguments for going down this track compelling and convincing. They really wanted a national agency to get the most out of combining their buying power!

It looked like I might have shot myself in the foot and set up a fantastic opportunity for one of the big national agencies. Fortunately for me, my director suggested I call one of the executive directors of Chandler Macleod Group. I called him and asked if they would consider subcontracting to us (that is, supplying temps to us that we could on-supply to David Jones). Being one of the big agencies, it seemed unlikely to me that they would agree to do this, as they could simply tender for the contract themselves with an excellent chance of winning due to their reputation. However, much to my delight, he agreed! That's how I was able to win the contract to supply David Jones with temp staff nationally.

Something I've noticed about people in the recruitment industry is that we isolate ourselves and are rarely inclined to work with our competitors. This seems to stem from a fear of our competitors 'stealing' our clients. My view has always been that if you can take my clients, then you deserve them as I obviously wasn't looking after them well enough. The pay-off for the industry of working together is far greater than the perceived dangers. In my experience with David Jones, it is clear that I would not have secured that contract had I not partnered with another agency. That's business I would not have had if I'd been too afraid of working with someone else or even asking them. It's preferable to get a smaller chunk of something big than get a whole chunk of nothing! When I could add David Jones to our client list, it undoubtedly opened other doors for me as well. As an interesting postscript: every contact we dealt with at David Jones was completely delightful. Its strong customer service culture extended not only to its customers but also its business partners.

In summary:

- Do not wait for your client to have a problem; use your expertise to identify and solve problems and you will usually get to deliver the solution.
- Open your mind to collaborating with other agencies to get more hours!

Selling the benefits of using temps

You need to be fully conversant with the benefits to clients of using temps, as these become your sales vocabulary. Some salespeople only talk about features, for example, 'We are the largest agency in the world', yet we know that people buy benefits.

The client doesn't really care that you have a large database, but they will care if you have temps on that database with skills in their industry, package or system, which is the benefit to them.

Features are something that your service has or does. For example, skills testing is something that your service does. Benefits are the result the client can expect from that particular feature. For example, you can guarantee that the temp can actually do what they say they can do as you've tested them.

An easy way of remembering the difference between features and benefits is to say, 'What we have is skills testing of all our temp staff [feature]; what that means for you is that you get the best skills match available for your needs [benefit]'. You can use this as a template until you're completely comfortable with selling benefits:

'What we have is [feature]; what that means for you is [benefit].'

Here are some benefits of using temps:

- The client only pays for the time the temp works, so it's more cost effective than hiring a permanent employee, where they have to pay for sick days, holiday pay, lunch hours and so on.
- There is less administration (which contributes to it being more cost effective) as the client will get one invoice, rather than having to be conversant with the correct award, issue a pay slip, calculate tax, pay the ATO, administer superannuation, pay payroll tax, deal with WorkCover and pay any other relevant statutory costs.
- 'Try before you buy' applies in a temp-to-perm situation. The client and temp can try each other out to see if it might be a good permanent match.
- Temps can be used to cope with increased sales or workload during a permanent headcount freeze by companies who do not include temps in their headcount.
- During uncertain economic times, such as the recession in the 1990s, the GFC in 2008 and the global pandemic in the early 2020s, companies can still run their businesses without the overhead of having permanent staff on their payroll. If things get tough, they can let the temps go without redundancy payments and in many cases with only an hour's notice (provided they have worked their day or shift minimum according to their relevant award, if applicable).
- During peak times companies can quickly hire staff as and when they need to, and possibly even rehire the same temps back when the need re-arises.
- Covering leave with temps means that staff don't come back to an increased workload that would defeat the benefits of taking leave. In the 1990s companies were retrenching so close to the bone that they suddenly saw sick days increase in their remaining staff due to stress and overwork, which cost them more time and money in the long run than if they had used temps to help out the

permanent staff. Since the global pandemic, the need for temps is strong because many people banked their holidays during the pandemic as they didn't want to use them when they couldn't go anywhere. Now companies are faced with staff wanting to take extended leave simultaneously, which leaves them short on people to actually run the business.

- Temp agencies provide a pool of skilled people available at short notice to cover for high-stress workplaces, such as contact centres where the absenteeism rate is high. Clients can make one call to the agency and replace their perm staff with temps for the duration of the period. To value-add for a client, I would have a number of temps already trained and inducted into their contact centre's procedures. This makes it easier for the client to get temps working quickly and also makes it harder for your competitors to get the job order as their temps won't be trained up.

- Staff management is done by the consultant. If you give the clients top service, they don't have to worry about absenteeism, holidays and other small issues that arise and have to be dealt with. This is part of the service and what the client pays you for: saving them time, effort and money. A number of clients would let their staff call me to tell me they weren't going to be in, and I would immediately organise a replacement temp before I advised the client of the roster for the day. Effectively the client gains an extra HR employee in you, which they only pay for through temp wages. This is excellent value for money for the client.

- There is continuous coverage without any downtime or loss of productivity, which saves the client money. If you offer an after-hours service, the client can call you and get a temp to start by the time their employee normally starts.

Chapter 7

Overcoming client objections

If you are new to the recruitment industry or lacking confidence in sales, it might seem that there are many different types of objections a client can come up with when you market temp recruitment services to them. However, after doing more than 10,000 hours of cold calling and telemarketing, I can confidently say that all the main objections can be grouped under the following three headings:

1. *Cost:* 'You're too expensive'
2. *Competitor:* 'We use another agency we're happy with', 'We do all our own recruitment' or 'We have a preferred supplier agreement (PSA)'
3. *Credibility:* 'We don't know if you are any good; why should we use you?'

From a confidence and comfort point of view, I found it a lot easier once I realised that objections can be grouped into these three categories. Once I had some different ways of overcoming each category, my confidence in picking up the phone not only soared, but I actually enjoyed making the calls! It had gone from a dreaded necessity to something I saw as a personal challenge and a bit of fun. It came down to knowing what to expect and being as prepared as I could be.

Let's take a look at some ways of overcoming the three types of objections.

Cost: 'You're too expensive'

When a client says 'you're too expensive', they want to drag you into a 'dollars and cents' conversation, which only looks at the hourly rate charged. On the face of it, your rate may be higher than your competitor's, but is your overall service actually more expensive? Remember, a temp is usually called in to perform a specific task. The more efficiently and effectively this is done, the better the value for the client. A 'cheaper' temp may be slower, less accurate and less proficient, which means they will take more hours to do the same job. They or someone else will have to spend time going back over the work to check it for accuracy. Someone will most likely have to spend more time showing them what to do, which takes that person away from their own job, for which there's a measurable cost as well. This is clearly a false economy for the client.

If your prospective client has previously had a temp with poor skills, they will not need to be convinced of the false economy. They may instead wonder how your temps are going to be different, which is really our third objection: 'How do I know you are any good at your job?'. This is about your credibility as a consultant. Understandably a client who has been burnt will be harder to convince to use a temp again.

Another scenario is that, when clients are used to getting second-rate temps, they may not even know what they can get in terms of competency and professionalism from a temp, because they think they are already getting the best available.

A good starting point when a client says 'You're too expensive' is for you to ask 'Compared to what?' We all know that if we buy a dress from Target it will be a very different price to one from Prada. One is not necessarily better than the other; just different. Likewise you can choose to be the Target or Prada of your niche in recruitment, but it is important that you make a conscious business decision. Imagine how confusing it would be for the client if they went to Target and had to pay Prada prices. So the 'Compared to what?' question is to ensure that your client is comparing apples with apples. As we are in a service industry, it is vital to focus on the service and value you provide when a comparison is being made. Because you have tested your temps' skills, you know exactly what the client is paying for. Because some agencies do not do skills testing, this provides an unequal comparison.

For example, your client may have a data entry assignment available for which they've been quoted $48.00 per hour, and you may quote $52.74 per hour. On the face of it, the other agency looks cheaper – but they may be sending someone who can do 8000 keystrokes per hour with 90% accuracy, whereas you're sending someone who can do 18,000 keystrokes per hour with 99% accuracy. Chances are that your temp will do the job in half the time and, because the client only pays for the time the temp works, they have in fact saved money by using your temp at the higher rate. Also, if you've provided them with a 20-minute call-back service, they've received better service as well as a better temp for less money. The better service equates to peace of mind for them, because they know a temp is booked and they can concentrate on doing their own job rather than worrying about whether a temp is available. Always ask what they are comparing your price to and what they are getting for it.

Case study: Samsung Electronics

Years ago I was marketing to Samsung Electronics. After calling them fortnightly for nine months with no result, the HR manager called me out of the blue with a data entry job order! He told me plainly that this was my one and only chance to prove myself to the organisation. I sent him a temp who did the job in half the allotted time at 100%

accuracy. When I called to do the four-hour check (which we'll discuss in chapter 9), the temp had already finished what they thought was going to be a full day's work! This was a memorable start to a long and mutually satisfying business partnership. Samsung became a major account for our entire company of 30 branches.

Here are the lessons I learnt from Samsung:

- Persistence really does pay off. By phoning every fortnight like clockwork, I made sure I was at the forefront of the client's mind when the time they needed a temp eventually came around.

- When you finally get an opportunity to supply, send the client your best! If you don't have someone good enough on the day, be brave and tell your client that you can't help. On the occasions I've had to do this, clients have always come back to me. They appreciate the honesty and integrity you display by not sending them someone rather than just sending them anyone and hoping for the best. Sometimes the clients had experienced another agency assuring them they had the right temp when in fact they didn't, and they realised that the agency was substandard as well as the temp. Sending your clients elsewhere may sound scary, but if you're giving best-practice service then it usually only serves to highlight just how good your service is!

- Do not oversell your temp's skills. Just be factual about what they tested at. In the Samsung example, I knew how good my temp was but just gave the manager the facts about her speed and accuracy when I booked her in. This allowed her to pleasantly surprise him and provided the opportunity to create a raving fan.

Competitor: 'We use another agency we're happy with'

My approach to this is: 'I'm so pleased to hear that you're experiencing good service. It's good to know that there are other professional people out there upholding the reputation of our industry. May I ask what it is in particular you like about your current supplier?' The specificity of their answers is critical: the client will tell you what they value in a temp service. Listen and note their answer without commenting. Then ask, 'Is there anything that they don't do that you wish they did?'

Again, listen carefully. Once they have told you what they like and dislike, you can jump in with your relevant features and benefits that specifically address what they value.

For example, the client might say, 'I really like that they always get back to me within a day of my placing a temp job order with them. Plus they also offer a good guarantee if the temp doesn't work out'.

It's critical that you listen carefully as the client is telling you what matters to them. This information sets you up nicely to highlight your service features and the attached benefits.

My reply to this would be, 'As speed and peace of mind are important to you, you might like to know that we offer a 20-minute call-back service, which means that within 20 minutes of your call, we will confirm the name of the temp with you'.

If the client highlights your competitor's guarantee and you know your guarantee is better, you can say, 'In terms of guarantee, our guarantee is that if you're not happy, you will get the first temp free, and the replacement temp's first seven hours are free as well. As far as I know, this is the best temp guarantee in the business. Honestly, we would be out of business if our clients had to call on our guarantee often, so we work very hard to ensure that we get it right the first time. Seeing as you mentioned the temp guarantee, is it something you've had to call upon quite a bit?'

You have to realise that when a client says 'we're happy' or 'we have a PSA' or anything like that, it's often to get you off the phone. It's what I call a fob off. So, it pays to dig a bit deeper. Your job is to understand your client's needs and concerns; ask questions to show interest and find out what's important to them.

Another way to tackle the fact that they already have an agency is to say, 'From time to time, if your supplier doesn't have the right person available, perhaps you'd like to give us a try? It can happen to the best of us that the skill you need on a particular day isn't readily available. How do you feel about using us as your back-up agency in a situation like that?'

Competitor: 'We do all our own recruitment'

When this objection is raised, some probing questions are good to find out a bit more. You can use a little preamble: 'That's great that you have in-house capacity to fill your own jobs'. Then, follow up with:

- 'Out of interest, how often do you have to call a casual in?'
- 'How many phone calls do you normally have to make to fill a shift or assignment?'
- 'What happens if none of your ex-employees or pool of casuals are available when you need them?'
- 'How would you fill the vacancy then?'
- 'Do you have an agency you use in that circumstance?'
- 'Would you consider using us?'

Competitor: We have a preferred supplier agreement (PSA)

In this case, ask the following:

- 'What type of staff does your PSA cover?' Usually PSAs only cover perms or temps. Or, they may be for a certain job family, such as accounting, while all other types of staff can be recruited from anyone. If the PSA doesn't cover what you provide, then proceed with your call as normal.
- 'Is it an official or unofficial agreement? If official, is it usually by invitation to tender or is it a public tender? When is it due for renewal? How can we get invited to tender as well?'

Again, this is about you asking intelligent, probing questions, which has the added side-effect of showing interest in them and of displaying your industry knowledge, so you can find an opening to discuss your service features and benefits. At the very least, you can find out when a tender opportunity may be available. If the tender renewal is nine to 12 months out, it's actually an ideal time for you to establish and build on some contacts in the company. At least you won't be a completely unknown entity to the company when the time comes for tendering.

You may even consider offering a free temp for a week (or a shorter timeframe) to one of the contacts you cultivate. This may be enough to get you an invitation to tender when the time comes around for tender renewal, as your company will be on record as having provided a temp in the past. Presumably you will also be able to provide an internal client testimonial from the grateful client who got the free temp! While this strategy may cost you a week's temp wages, it's a relatively small investment to make to have a decent chance at securing a major PSA, which may be worth thousands (if not hundreds of thousands) of dollars.

Also ask if you can provide them with temps if the suppliers on their PSA can't supply. Often this is the case, as PSA rates may be so low that well-qualified people are unwilling to fill the jobs (particularly in a skills-short market), or the agency may simply not have someone with that particular skill set available the day the client requires it. Usually this means you can supply at your normal hourly rates rather than at the rates prescribed in the agreement. Being a back-up agency can open doors for you when the tender comes around for renewal as you will have proven both the quality of your service and the quality of your temps.

Case study: Australian Administration Services

The first time I tendered to supply Australian Administration Services (AAS) with temps I wasn't successful, but we became their back-up agency. During the year of that 12-month contract, their preferred supplier couldn't keep up with filling the orders, so we got more and more of the work thanks to our speed and the quality of temps we delivered. When the contract next went out for tender, we were in an extremely strong position as we had many successful runs on the board and had established a strong relationship with AAS managers and employees. This, I believe, was a strong contributing factor to us winning the next tender process.

Credibility: We don't know if you are any good or why should we use you

This is about ability and credibility – either yours or your company's. A good way to overcome this objection is to use a case study or tell a story (which, by the way, is the most effective way of transferring information as people remember stories). It may be a story about another company in the prospect's industry – that is, their competitor – who used to use someone else but now uses you as you were able to source the specialist employees they needed. If you have a testimonial from that company, even better!

I'm a huge fan of testimonials as they provide social proof that you can in fact do the job. They have always worked well, but with the prolific use of social media today they have become even more effective as a marketing tool. Whether you like it or not, people will post, tweet and review how you stack up. As well as Google reviews, there are platforms that allow temps to rate your service, which is there for all to see.

If you have clients who 'love your guts', do you have a written testimonial or LinkedIn recommendation from them? If not, why not? With a folder of testimonials on hand, you can confidently say to a client, 'I could tell you how good we are, but it's probably more credible for you to hear it from some of our clients/temps. So, at a time that suits you, I'd like to come and spend 20 minutes with you to give you an opportunity to tell me how you prefer to work with a recruitment agency, and you can view our testimonials at the same time. That way you can see first-hand who we deal with'.

This approach allows you to organically ask for a client visit. Notice how I don't ask a closed question: 'Can I show you our testimonials at a meeting?' That would more likely have elicited a 'no'. Also notice how I used the word 'you' more than the word 'I'? Remember, in selling and influencing, it's not about you, but always about your client. Let your language reflect that.

'You' and 'yours' are two sales power words to use frequently. Bearing this in mind also forces you to think about why it's in the client's interest to agree to what you're suggesting, which is another way of ensuring you're focusing on the benefits for them.

Overcoming objections is a special skill set that can be learnt through practice, focus and sales training. Practice is the most important aspect. Malcolm Gladwell's *Outliers* gives many examples of how the average person with dedication to practice trumps the person who has more talent but does not devote the time to practice.

I learnt how to overcome objections effectively by making thousands of calls and visits. I had to make 30 calls per day, which took roughly eight hours, as I didn't have any jobs to fill. Forty hours per week × 48 weeks = 1920 hours per annum. It would only take a little over five years to achieve Gladwell's 10,000 hours at that rate. In fact I did get a lot busier filling jobs once the temp desk took off, which was roughly six months after making those 30 calls a day – but after 18 years working directly in recruitment, I know I have devoted a lot more than 10,000 hours to making sales calls!

By starting your calls today, you ensure that you're well on the path to your own mastery. By using the ideas in this book, you will be able to shave off some time – but reading about them is not enough. Practice makes permanent!

Chapter 8

What to pay and charge for temps

Temp rates are usually governed by awards or an enterprise or site agreement. Award rates are most common, although in reality you will most likely have to pay market rates, particularly in a skills-short market.

Depending on the type of temps you supply, you will have to look up the relevant award for that category to determine the correct pay rate.

Since 1 January 2010 we have had modern awards in Australia; a list of more than 100 awards can be found at fairwork.gov.au/employment-conditions/awards.

Here you can search for the award that's applicable to your temps. As I've used clerical staff as my example, I will use the Clerks – Private Sector Award 2020 here for illustration.

As awards are constantly changing, you need to keep abreast of any and all changes. For example, during the global pandemic the minimum shift under some awards was changed to two hours where it is normally a three-hour minimum.

While you may have a payroll person or company that pays your temps and invoices your clients, you still need to know the basic award conditions that apply to your temps as your temps and clients will need to access this information at some point. Learning about awards and how to interpret them is one way you can provide expertise to your clients.

The Clerks – Private Sector Award 2020 covers all clerical employees in Australia unless they are covered by another award specific to their industry (as listed here):

- the Aged Care Award 2010
- the Airline Operations – Ground Staff Award 2020
- the Airport Employees Award 2020
- the Alpine Resorts Award 2020
- the Animal Care and Veterinary Services Award 2020
- the Banking, Finance and Insurance Award 2020
- the Black Coal Mining Industry Award 2020
- the Business Equipment Award 2020
- the Contract Call Centres Award 2020
- the Educational Services (Post-Secondary Education) Award 2020
- the Educational Services (Schools) General Staff Award 2020
- the Fitness Industry Award 2020
- the General Retail Industry Award 2020
- the Health Professionals and Support Services Award 2020
- the Higher Education Industry – General Staff – Award 2020
- the Hospitality Industry (General) Award 2020
- the Legal Services Award 2020
- the Market and Social Research Award 2020
- the Rail Industry Award 2020
- the Restaurant Industry Award 2020
- the Sporting Organisations Award 2020
- the Telecommunications Services Award 2020.

Here are the basic points in the Clerks – Private Sector Award that were correct at the time of writing:

- Ordinary hours are 38 hours per week up to four weeks or 38 hours per week as agreed between the employer and employee.
- Ordinary hours can be worked between 7 am and 7 pm Monday to Friday and between 7 am and 12.30 pm Saturday.
- The employer must pay a casual loading of 25% on top of the minimum hourly rate for a casual or temp employee.
- The casual loading is 25% on top of the equivalent hourly rate for a permanent employee. So you need to know what the permanent weekly wage is for an adult:

  Level 1, year 1 permanent weekly wage: $861.40

  As a normal week is 38 hours, you divide $861.40 by 38 to find the hourly rate:

  $861.40 ÷ 38 = $22.67 per hour

  To determine the casual rate, you add 25% casual loading:

  $22.67 + 25% = $28.34 per hour

  This is for a Level 1 employee, which is the lowest level in this award.

- Current adult (21 years and older) casual pay rates are between $28.34 and $39.14 per hour depending on what level the temp is classified as under the award.
- Shifts are a three-hour minimum, which means when you send a temp out you must pay them for three hours even if they only work for two. This charge is passed on to your client as it's an award requirement. I would normally ask the client if they have some extra work in order to utilise the temp for the full three hours as they have to pay for them anyway.
- Overtime for work done on Monday to Saturday for the first two hours beyond 38 hours in a week is at 175% of the minimum

hourly rate. After the first two hours this increases to 225% of the minimum hourly rate.

· Sunday all day is at 225% of the minimum hourly rate.

· Public holidays all day is at 275% of the minimum hourly rate.

· The temp is entitled to a minimum of ten hours off between consecutive days' work, or they must be paid 200% of the minimum hourly rate until they are released from duty and then have a minimum of ten consecutive hours off duty.

· Adults under this award are 21 years and older. If younger than 21 years they must be paid according to their age as stipulated in the award.

· The temp is entitled to have a meal provided or a meal allowance of $16.91 if they work more than 1.5 hours of overtime without 24 hours' notice. If they work more than four hours' overtime without 24 hours' notice, a further meal allowance of $13.54 is payable.

The above is correct at the time of writing and according to my interpretation of the modern award pertaining to clerks. It is your responsibility to keep up-to-date with award changes, which usually happen once a year. To make it easy, you can enter the relevant award name as a keyword into Google alerts and be notified whenever there's any news about that particular award.

Determining a charge rate

Using the Level 1 pay rate of $28.34, we could use the following formula to work out a charge rate to the client:

Pay rate + on-costs + markup = charge rate

On-costs depend on where you're supplying the temps, as they vary from state to state and, of course, from country to country.

Let's use New South Wales as an example. On-costs include 10.5% superannuation, 5.45% payroll tax and 2% workers compensation (this is an average estimate; the exact rate will depend on which industry they work in). You could add 1% for professional indemnity and public liability insurances. So, you can calculate your total as follows:

$$10.5 + 5.45 + 2 + 1 = 18.95\%$$

You could round this up to 19% in on-costs. If you choose to use a 30% markup, then your charge rate would be as follows:

$$\$28.34 + 19\% + 30\% = \$43.84 \text{ per hour per weekday}$$

It costs you $28.34 + 19% = $33.72 per hour to have the person out working – this includes the rate paid to the temp plus all the relevant on-costs.

Your gross margin per hour would be as follows:

$$\$43.84 - \$33.72 = \$10.12$$

If that temp worked a 38-hour week, your weekly gross margin would be $384.56.

I like to work on a higher markup – for example, 40% to 45% – which would make the charge rates look like this:

40% markup:

$$\$28.34 + 19\% + 40\% = \$47.21 \text{ with a gross margin of}$$
$$\$13.49 \text{ per hour or } \$512.62 \text{ per week}$$

45% markup:

$$\$28.34 + 19\% + 45\% = \$48.90 \text{ with a gross margin of}$$
$$\$15.18 \text{ per hour or } \$576.86 \text{ per week}$$

It's far preferable to use a formula like this than work on a fixed-dollar margin. I have seen some companies adopt a fixed margin of $7.00 per hour regardless of what type of temp they supply. The problem with this is that the higher-skilled temps are scarcer and therefore harder to find, which means the margin the client pays you for sourcing, attracting and managing those higher-skilled temps isn't aligned with the amount of work you're investing in filling their assignment.

For example, if you advertise for contact centre operators, you may get lots of applicants with varying degrees of experience. You may be able to use a large number of those with excellent work histories, as you can use your influencing skills to persuade the client to hire them on a lower or trainee level. If on the other hand your client needs a contact centre supervisor with a minimum three to five years' experience in the insurance industry, the search is likely to be extensive, as many of these people may not be available for temp work. If you use the formula with a markup as a percentage component, then your dollar margin will be proportional to the level of temp skill required.

Payrolling a temp

On occasion clients may want you to payroll a temp, or you may find that a company has a decent-size pool of their own casuals and you can offer to payroll them. A payrolling service is different to supplying a temp in that the client has sourced the temp or casual that they want to hire. There can be various reasons why they prefer the casual to be on an agency's payroll, including headcount restrictions and avoiding the hassle of having to administer wages, superannuation, workers compensation and other costs. Another reason can be that they simply want the skills of the casual but not the hassle of their day-to-day management. The relationship that they have with the casual changes as it is no longer an employer and employee situation. The casual is hired as a temp through the agency, which then on-hires that temp to the client.

The benefits to the client of the on-hire arrangement as opposed to a direct hire arrangement are pretty clear and easy for you to 'sell' to your clients:

- The client only pays one invoice rather than being responsible for administering statutory costs as well as the temp's entitlements.
- The relationship with the temp is at arm's length, although there are joint work health and safety (WHS) obligations.

- Management of the temp is carried out by the temp agency, including dealing with performance issues, hiring and firing.

What to charge for payrolling a temp

While you didn't recruit the temp for the client, you are performing an administrative function for the client and taking on the risk of that temp as your employee. That said, the charge rate may be different to someone you did source. Clients expect that the recruitment industry in Australia will charge a lower hourly rate for payrolling a temp than for a standard temp. So, instead of using our previous formula (pay rate + on-costs + markup = charge rate), the formula you use might look more like this:

Pay rate + on-costs + 25% = charge rate

For example, if the award pay rate is $28.34:

$28.34 + 19% + 25% = $42.15 per hour per weekday
with a gross margin of $8.44 per hour or $320.72 per week

The lowest margin I've heard of for a payrolling service was an hourly margin of $2.00 for a blue-collar temp. In my opinion this is far too low for a blue-collar worker as they are often in higher- risk jobs, such as driving forklifts or trucks.

If you come across a client with many of their own casuals on their books, you may want to market this service to them. If successful, your hours will grow, but your average hourly margin will of course be affected. That's why it's important to focus on number of hours *and* average margin when growing your temp desk. We all know of recruitment companies that have 'bought' business by offering unsustainably low margins. This might be part of their strategy for winning certain employer brands as clients, but in the long term, this is not good business practice. You end up doing a lot of work for little or no return, or you get a workers compensation claim that instantly decimates your profits.

Pricing considerations

Here are some more things to consider with regard to pricing:

- While there are award rates, temps are usually paid well above those rates in a skill-short market. In this type of market, temps need to be highly skilled and there is fierce competition to get the best temps. Clients need to be educated on the difference between award rates, which tell us the absolute minimum rates temps have to be paid, and market rates, which is what their skills and experience command in any given temp market.

- Remember when I used the analogy of a Prada dress and a Target dress, or a Mercedes and a Toyota? One is not necessarily better than the other, but each of these brands serves a different demographic and purpose and, therefore, sits in a different price category. Before you decide what your percentage markup is, think about the temp recruitment industry and where you want to pitch your temp services. Are you the Mercedes or the Toyota of temp agency providers?

- Never compete on price, on dollars and cents; it's a race to the bottom of the lowest, untenable margins and lowers the service levels in the industry. Always compete on value. It is with value in mind that you decide where you want to pitch your temp services.

- If you also provide a perm placement or other complementary recruitment services, your temp service offering needs to be aligned to them. So, if you offer top-of-the-line perm recruitment services at 20% to 25% fees, your temp hourly charge rates should also be in the higher range, i.e. 45% to 50% markup. Incidentally I have always been among the most expensive in terms of temp hourly rates. My rationale for this was as follows:

  - We had the best temps, as the benchmarks in terms of hard, measurable skills were set high for people wanting to temp for us.

- Our service was the best: 20-minute call-back service, and treating clients with honesty and integrity.
- We had the best temp guarantee in the business, so there was no risk to the clients.
- My experience tells me unequivocally that clients do not complain about the rates if they are happy with the temp and your service. They only complain if you give them $2-shop value and charge them top dollar. So, if you decide to charge them top dollar, make sure your service and temps cannot be faulted!

· If a client asks you for a discount, please reread chapter 7, specifically the section about overcoming the price/cost objection. One good way of growing your hours is to ask the client how much temp business they have, as you'd consider a 'bulk' discount (like in the David Jones case study I outlined in chapter 6). Think very carefully about giving the client a discount without blinking, though, as it's nearly impossible to raise your rates again unless you change your service offering to include a lot more 'value'.

· Consider how much margin you are prepared to do payrolling for. Why do you want to do it? Is it to get a foot in the door of that particular client company so you can supply them with other, more lucrative recruitment services?

Business partnership or master–servant relationship?

It's critical to learn to get comfortable with discussing rates with your clients. Every time you confirm a temp, you need to confirm the rate verbally and in an email. Upon booking you will say, for example:

'I've booked Julia for you and the rate for her is $48.98 per hour per weekday up to 38 hours per week or 7.6 hours per day. For anything over this, overtime applies, as per the Clerks – Private Sector Award 2020. She will bring a time sheet with her, or you can access our online time sheet to verify her hours on a weekly basis so we can pay her correctly and invoice you accordingly. The verified time sheet needs to be with us by 10 am on Monday mornings.'

Again, the more specific you are in setting expectations, the fewer problems will appear later on. If you rely on your client to read an email with your hourly rate, this can easily fall through the cracks. The client can claim they didn't have time to read it, or they would have raised the issue of the hourly rate with you. It's extremely messy to discuss rates once a temp has already started on their assignment, as you're bound by the rate quoted to the temp. You are the expert in the temp recruitment field, so you must be confident of your abilities and stand up for your rates and service. Imagine going to a medical specialist and saying, 'No, I don't agree with your diagnosis and I think your fee is unreasonable'! This is unthinkable; we simply accept that they are the experts and it's not the type of service that people negotiate on.

Having said that, there may be situations where you actually want to negotiate with a client – for example, if they use multiple temps and you want a bigger slice of their business. In this case, ask them what their usage is in terms of dollar spend, temp numbers, type of temps and, most importantly, whether they are willing to give you this business. Once you have this information, you can make an informed decision about what you're prepared to sacrifice in percentage markup to gain the extra hours.

Most importantly, remember that negotiations involve give and take from both parties. If the client doesn't give you anything in the form of information or more temp job orders, but you agree to give them a lower hourly rate, the previously equal business relationship has suddenly turned into a master–servant relationship: they command and you respond by jumping however high they want you to jump. Not only have you lost money as you've had to lower your margin, you've also lost your credibility. If you don't believe in and fight for your expertise and rates, why would the client?

The way we think about our job and our role determines our behaviour, which can be a strength or a weakness. For example, let's say a new client calls you with your very first job order. When you call to book in the temp, Joe, and quote the rate, the client tells you that it's too high and they want a $2.00 per hour discount.

What are your options here?

1. You can reduce your margin to secure the job.

2. You can explain that your rate is determined by market rates and you've booked them Joe with x, y, z skills.

3. You can ask for a meeting to gather information about their total temp usage so you can give them preferential rates for exclusivity.

4. You can offer them David at the $2.00 lower rate, but explain carefully the difference in David's and Joe's skills; for example, David may have less experience in that particular skill set and therefore may take slightly longer to complete the work. Explain that David commands a lower hourly rate, which is what enables you to offer him out at the cheaper charge rate. Also explain that you would never try to underpay Joe according to market rates as this may cause resentment and prevent him from agreeing to work for your client next time.

As per your policy, you always book the best person available, but if your client insists on having a say in the rate charged, let them decide which temp they want. Most clients will actually choose the more expensive person when they understand the difference in skill set. When it comes down to actual, real people rather than just speaking theoretically about skill levels, the client's understanding of the difference improves markedly.

The conversation always needs to be about value and not dollars and cents. I consider it a big part of a recruiter's job to educate clients on market conditions. After all, it's your area of expertise, not theirs; be generous with your knowledge and share what you know with your clients.

Which of the above options would you choose? I would either choose option 3 or a combination of 4 and 3 to get this booking confirmed, and then work on cementing the relationship with the client for the long term. Option 1 is by far the worst option for you. I suspect some clients use requesting a discount as a 'test' to see how willing you are to defend your expertise. Sadly I know that many recruiters automatically say 'yes' when they are asked to drop their rates, which in turn causes them to feel resentment towards the client. In my view this situation is completely their own doing. They need to become better at advocating for their own and their temps' strengths. You probably know the feeling yourself when you come across someone who is knowledgeable; you feel you're in good hands, and you're usually willing to pay for that expertise and the peace of mind that comes with it.

How to pay your temps and charge your clients

Let's take a look at some best-practice methods of paying your temps and charging your clients.

Time sheets and pay

The Clerks – Private Sector Award 2020 provides that employees must be paid weekly or fortnightly – but as you only get paid when your temp has been paid, the most common process is to pay the temps weekly. As on-hire staff, temps don't have to adhere to the client company's pay week, so you can decide when a week starts and finishes. When I worked at Ecco, our temp week went from Thursday to Wednesday. It was up to the temps to get their signed time sheet to us on time, which was by Friday at 5 pm. Most agencies have weeks that go from Monday to Sunday now. Whatever your week is, you have to allow enough time for the time sheet information to be collated and pays to be done in time for the payment deadline. Please check your specific award to see if there are any particular days your temps have to be paid by.

If you are supplying a contractor – that is, someone who is being paid as a company with their own Australian Business Number (ABN) – you should be able to negotiate when they are to be paid. If they work as a sole trader, you must treat them as an on-hire staff – just like a temp.

It's very important to emphasise to the temps at their initial interview that it's their responsibility to get their time sheets authorised and forwarded to you via email, app or hard copy by a certain time. Otherwise you may end up spending many hours chasing your temps for time sheets, which actually inhibits you from growing your hours. The only line to take on this is to say that if their time sheet isn't in, they won't get paid – but also tell them that it greatly inconveniences the client company, which may have a certain budget to be spent within a certain time.

Here is a good way to ask temps to send you their authorised time sheets on time:

> 'Our working week goes from Monday to Sunday. If your working week finishes on a Friday, you need to get the client to sign your time sheet or authorise it via email before then so you can get paid on time. If I don't get the time sheet by Friday 5 pm, you will miss the pay run. If you need to work over the weekend, your deadline for getting the time sheet to us is Monday morning at 10 am. If your manager is away or in a meeting, call me on Friday and let me know so I can get authorisation from someone else for you to get paid. If your assignment finishes on a different day to Friday, make sure you get your approved time sheet to me before you leave the job.'

Most recruitment companies pay their temps first and then invoice their clients with a copy of the approved time sheet attached. If you don't get the time sheet on time, you can't pay the temp, which means you can't invoice the client, which also means you can't count those hours in your weekly billings! Therefore it's absolutely imperative that you get your temps trained to be very disciplined with getting their time sheets in on time.

Remember, the successful recruiter is always juggling the three critical tasks on a daily basis. If you have to waste time chasing time sheets, it's precious time away from the three critical tasks! I've known some consultants who spend half a day chasing time sheets – it keeps them occupied but with a totally non-productive task, as the work for those hours has already been done and it doesn't directly generate any more hours.

As a temp consultant, you walk a very fine line between being your temps' employer and confidante, but you can't get too chummy with them or they won't respect you, which means they won't do what you need them to do at the times you need them to.

Also remember that specificity is gold. Be specific when you ask for something. For example, say, 'Please have your time sheet to me by 5 pm. If you can't, then let me know by 5 pm'. It's far more precise than saying, 'Get your manager to sign your time sheet at the end of the day and email it to me ASAP'. By being specific, you leave no room for misunderstandings or excuses! If a temp doesn't do what you expected, examine what your instructions were. Either you weren't specific enough or they aren't good at taking instruction. If the latter is the case, you have to consider whether they are suitable to work as a temp, as their job is to take instructions from various people in a multitude of assignments. You want people who can quickly grasp instructions and comply.

Invoicing clients

Invoicing a client can be done in different ways. You may have an integrated system where you can log a job with the correct pay and charge rates and, once a temp has been paid, it automatically generates an online and/or PDF invoice. Alternatively, you may outsource this function to an external provider, in which case they may chase the time sheet for you and invoice the clients.

Whichever way you do it, you have to ensure the clients are invoiced immediately. Your temps are already paid, which means your cash is outstanding. As clients understand you're paying the temps upfront, you can ask for seven-day payment on all temp invoices. Seven days is standard procedure in the industry anyway. Be on the watch for temp invoices that don't get paid, because companies in trouble have been known to use temp agencies to fund their business. When you deal with a new temp client, you must state upfront that, because you pay your temps on a weekly basis, all temp invoices are payable within seven days, and ask if this can be adhered to. If they say they only pay invoices in 30 days, I would add another 2.5% markup to the hourly rate to take this into account. If you give a client the option, they will usually go with the seven days and lower hourly rate. If you're dealing with a large company or government organisation where their accounts payable runs are fairly rigid, you may decide that you will accept different payment terms to the seven days. I would only do it for a large client – one that uses many temps at once – and only if I get the business exclusively. What you end up doing needs to be guided by your company policy, your client agreement and your cashflow situation.

Funding your temp payroll

Now that you know you need to pay your temps upfront before invoicing your clients, you need to decide how best to fund your temp desk. While having a temp desk is very lucrative and guaranteed money in the bank, you do need to have working capital to start one up.

Here are some different funding options:

· You have cash deposits that you can use for this purpose.

· You borrow money from a bank to fund your temp payroll.

· You use factoring (also known as debtor finance). This is a process whereby you 'sell' your invoices to a bank or financial provider for 75% to 90% of the invoice value. The bank or provider then collects the money owed on the invoice and pays you the balance of the invoice value after deducting commission and fees. If, after a certain time (such as 30 days), the client hasn't paid, the factoring business will pay the recruitment company and start collection proceedings against the client.

· You outsource to an external service provider, who will do all back-office functions including paying your temps for a percentage of your margin or a flat fee.

Seek professional financial advice to determine the best option for you, as every business (and business owner) is different.

Chapter 9

Best-practice service for temps

As a temp consultant you have two equally important client groups:

1. Your temps, without whom you can't supply any client companies

2. Your client companies, without whom you can't provide any work for your temps.

When you think about your job in this way, it is obvious that both groups require dedication and care. I have seen recruiters treat their temps with disdain and a lack of respect, and then they wonder why the temps don't feel any loyalty towards them. Loyalty is earned and given voluntarily. It is not something you can demand.

Over the last few years quality temps have been hard to source, and therefore they've become more 'valuable' than clients. If there is a shortage of talent, finding and retaining great people becomes paramount to all employers – and this includes you as a temp employer.

To be the best temp recruiter, you need to be able to attract temps to you – which is only the beginning. Then there is the process of earning their trust and loyalty so they will do anything for you and be your ambassador to client companies and other temps. Every interaction you have with a temp is an opportunity to cement and deepen that relationship.

A typical chain of temp interactions

With this in mind, let's take a look at a typical chain of interactions with a new temp.

1. The temp emails or uploads their CV

Ideally you should respond to all CVs within 24 hours. If you get a walking dollar temp, they probably won't even last that long. Have you ever called a temp only to discover they've already found work? That's because you didn't respond quickly or enthusiastically enough. To ensure you treat every applicant with respect, you need to respond – whether their application is successful or not. For example:

> 'Thank you for your application. In this instance, you haven't been successful, but we wish you all the best in your job search. Please feel free to apply to us in future for any other vacancies.'

Or:

> 'Due to the high volume of responses, our aim is to get back to you within 24 hours of this email. Thank you for your interest in this position and your patience.'

I recommend that you dedicate three one-hour time slots per day to look at and respond to your emails – for example, at 8.30 am, 12 pm and 4.30 pm. When you do review CVs, decide whether each applicant goes into your 'yes', 'no' or 'maybe' pile. Call all the 'yes' people immediately and arrange interviews with them in the next 24 hours. Send the 'thanks, but no thanks' standard response to the people in the 'no' pile. Email the 'maybe' people with the 'we will get back to you within 24 hours' response.

2. You interview the temp

Naturally you will already have explained to the temp the format of the interview, the duration and what to expect. If you are going to be administering tests, tell them in advance so they allow for this in their parking time. The interview is for you to establish the temp's skills and determine whether they are a good fit for your temp team in terms of the benchmarking you have put in place (as described in chapter 5). If you decide you can use the temp, you need to lay down the ground rules of what they can expect from you and, likewise, what you expect from them. If you can't use the temp, it's appropriate you tell them why, as it may be something they can fix. This is where the consulting part of 'temp consultant' comes in. Be generous with your expertise and actually consult. If you don't, you've chosen to be a job filler, which is a long way from consulting.

Should you interview face-to-face or via video call? Since the global pandemic, recruiters have gotten used to virtual interviews, but when possible you should still interview face-to-face as you are building a workforce. You need to build trust and loyalty. While this can be done virtually, it is not the same!

Case study: Amy (temp applicant)

Years ago I had an American applicant – let's call her Amy – register with me for temp work. Amy was highly qualified and had recently been a general manager for a luxury hotel chain in the United States. Amy had almost everything – the right attitude, common sense, intelligence and professionalism – but unfortunately she didn't have experience using the software that most clients had converted to. I told Amy this and she asked if I would be able to find her some temp work if she did a course in the software. I said, 'Absolutely', as that was the only element needed to make her a walking dollar temp.

Amy went and did the course, and I sent her as my very first temp to Merck Sharp & Dohme (MSD; remember the MD I called late on a Friday night?). Unbeknownst to me at the time, Amy had been to another agency before she came to me. The consultant there had told her they would find her work, but she never heard from them again. It turned out it was the same agency that MSD had used for ten years! While I don't think the agency set out to treat her poorly, they should have known that they couldn't place her without skills in the market-preferred software. However, rather than communicate this vital nugget of local market information, they chose to leave it, with unfortunate and lasting consequences for themselves.

Amy was such a good temp that she was kept on at MSD long past the initial booking dates. During this time, she would tell everyone that the other agency had treated her in an unprofessional way and that only I had been honest enough to tell her what she needed to upskill herself and ultimately find work. Without knowing the backstory, I had inadvertently put the best ambassador into MSD that I could have hoped for.

Think about how you treat your temps and applicants as they can be your best brand ambassadors or your worst detractors. While looking after your brand has always been important, in the current climate of social media, it is critically important. People can trash a brand quicker than you can bat an eyelid.

Of course, it's easy to tell people the truth when it relates to their skill level – for example, they're not fast enough or advanced enough. It's more difficult when it's about something they can't change, or something they may consider to be discriminatory. In these cases, you must tread cautiously.

Case study: Bob (candidate for a temp-to-perm position)

One time I had an excellent contact centre operator – let's call him Bob – apply for a temp-to-perm job with one of my electronics clients. Bob had solid contact centre experience and was an outgoing, caring person – just the kind you want in your contact centre. During our interview, though, all I could do was stare at his eyebrow ring. I knew that this particular electronics client would take one look at Bob and the client interview would be over, regardless of his skill set.

I didn't want to waste Bob's, my client's or my time – plus Bob was such a good temp that I really wanted him to work for us. At the end of the interview, I said to Bob, 'I think you're great. The only concern I have is that the manager at the company you've applied for will probably ask you to take out your eyebrow ring. I personally don't have a problem with the eyebrow ring, but if I don't give you this information, it will diminish your chances of getting that job and then I wouldn't be doing my job properly. How do you feel about that? If you'd prefer not to work there, I have another client – a funky young credit-card company – and they would warmly welcome you into their team. What do you think?' Bob thanked me for my honesty and said he was interested in the credit-card company position. As predicted, that client loved him and Bob ended up securing a permanent job there.

In my experience, if you speak with sincerity and from a place of caring, you can say almost anything. What can get you into trouble is saying things in a judgemental or non-caring manner. Always make it clear that it's not your personal opinion, but you're concerned about their chances of securing the job and how comfortable they will be working in an environment where they may stand out or even be singled out. When people talk about a company 'culture', this is one of the things that matters. Culture refers to 'the way we do things around here' and how you present is very much part of that.

Also be careful that you don't impose your own standards on your clients. A recruiter I was once working with told me she had a lot of trouble finding suitable temps. When I dug a bit deeper, it turned out that she wanted her temps to be a size eight and to wear Cue suits! After discussing these extremely narrow criteria, she could see that perhaps these standards were not only too high, but that in fact some of her clients would feel uncomfortable having a temp dressed like this when it clashed with their own more relaxed dress code.

At the end of the day, it's not what you like that matters but what your clients like and expect. Your job is to identify their criteria and meet them. If in doubt, it's better for your temp to be overdressed than underdressed on the first day. It's preferable if you have physically been to the company's offices so you can get a first-hand feel for the culture.

Your job is to ensure that the temp fits in and feels comfortable and the client accepts the temp as one of their own team.

3. You book the temp for an assignment

It's important to be really *specific* with assignment details every time you book a temp, but the first time, you also need to reiterate some of the 'rules' you mentioned at the interview. Consider the rule that if they are sick, late or need any time off, they are to call you. To maintain control of the assignment and relationship with your temp and client, all requests, information and approvals need to go through you. Tell the temp that you are there for them. If everything goes through you, you can and will protect them from potentially unpleasant situations when it could be the client's word against theirs.

Issues can occur even with something as simple as asking for a day off. The temp might ask the client directly for a day off and while the client agrees, they resent it and would in fact have said 'no' if you, as the consultant, had enquired on the temp's behalf. This can then jeopardise continuation of the assignment or prevent the client from requesting that same temp back. The temp will naturally feel unfairly treated, arguing that the client could have just said 'no', but the reality is that some people, including clients, don't like confrontation and may say 'yes' just to avoid it.

The point is that the whole situation could have been averted if the request had come through you. You might already have known that the week in question was particularly busy at the client's company, so you could have advised your temp that it was unlikely they would get the time off then. Or, the client would have simply told you 'no'. Alternatively, the client might have said 'yes' if you could organise a replacement – which brings us back to the importance of you having control over the assignment and the hours associated with it. If you have temps taking time off without your knowledge, you miss out on the opportunity to replace them – and the first you will know about it is when you see the time sheet or it is missing altogether. This makes you look bad to the client as you don't know what your temps are doing, and it results in you losing hours and, therefore, money. The result is that the client receives bad service from you as they were left without a temp for the day. And you weren't even aware!

Also remind your temp of the 'rules' about when and how their time sheet is to be submitted. Remember, specificity is gold. Be specific about the day and exact time. The more specific you are, the less likely things will go wrong, as the instructions are clear and not open to multitudes of interpretations. People can have the right intention but not the same interpretation as you. Eliminate the potential for misunderstandings.

You may want to reiterate 'rules' around mobile phone and internet usage. Note that your agency's rules may differ from the client's. If they do, you need to be specific about which rules the temp should abide by. My view is that the temp works for you and is on-hired to the client company, and as such needs to abide by your rules rather than the client company's. For instance, the client company may say it's okay to use the internet for personal use if there isn't much work to do, but your advice is that, if there isn't much work to do, the temp should ask for more work. Your advice needs to prevail, as the level of work is open to interpretation. The client pays for the temp to work, therefore the temp needs to work, or at least ask for work. Perhaps the rule is that the temp calls you if they can't find any work. You can then check with the client to verify that there really isn't anything for the temp to do. This avoids any misunderstandings where the client thinks your temp is being lazy on the job. Again, you can tell your temp that this covers their back as you are looking out for them.

Apart from the 'rules', you need to tell the temp exactly what they will be doing on the assignment, who they will be reporting to, the hours and location of work, the duration of the assignment, the pay rate and who will conduct the WHS induction. In addition, it's good temp service to communicate practical information such as where to park, where to get lunch, any company rules and what the dress code is.

4. Regular contact while on assignment

Once on an assignment, you need to be in regular contact with your temp. Remember, they work for you and you have an obligation to ensure all is well with them. Remind them that if the client changes their duties, it may entitle them to a higher rate. Ask them to call you weekly at a time that suits them, because if you call them they may be in the middle of something or the boss might be right next to them, meaning they can't speak freely. However, it can still be good to set a timeframe. For example, you might say, 'As I will be speaking to the client on a weekly basis, can you please call me by 12 pm on Thursdays? That way I can raise any issues you have when I speak to your manager on Thursday afternoons'. Remember that most people will agree to do something if you tell them how they will benefit from doing it. Simply commanding rarely works if they can't see the reason for it. Or, worse, they may object to being 'bossed around', which creates the wrong impression of the relationship you want to foster with them.

5. Before the assignment comes to an end

Don't wait until the assignment finishes to start working on the next job for your temp. As you are in weekly contact with your temp and your client, you can and should use these calls to extend the assignment if both parties are happy. Or, if an extension is not possible, you need to tell your temp that you will do everything you can to find them a job to start when this job finishes or they are next available. Being in control and knowing the timelines will enable you to keep your temps working and prevent them from being booked by other agencies. Your temps are your assets. It's very difficult for you to build and grow your hours if you lose your assets. Clients love getting the same temps back – they are more efficient because they already know the ropes of the client company. You cannot offer this service if you lose your temps to other agencies. Worst of all, your competitor may actually offer your temp back to your client! That is heartbreaking and money down the drain.

6. While your temp is out of work

During this period, it's vital that you keep an open line of communication with your temp. They need to know you're looking for work for them and you need to know what they are doing – for example, if they are actively pursuing other avenues of work. Only speaking to your temps when you have something for them will mean that they are unlikely to be available to do the assignment for you. This differs greatly to how a perm recruiter operates: they will contact the candidate if and when a perm job becomes available. A temp recruiter must find work for their temps and not leave them languishing, plus they may rely on you to pay their bills!

7. Visiting the temp in ongoing assignments

You can visit your temps as well as speaking to them on a weekly basis. It's not 'set and forget' when you place a temp. The pay-off for you is that the temp feels important, and they will also become your best source of information. As they are working on the inside of the client company, they can tell you about projects coming up, resignations, product launches or new system implementations – in short, other opportunities for you to provide services, thereby increasing your value to the client, which in turn will deepen your relationship with the client. This information-gathering will happen organically as you ask what's happening in the company. Temps will also want to tell you about other temps in the company from your competitors. There may be other decision-makers using temps who you haven't yet made contact with or were even aware of.

Service matters

Case study: Boral Masonry

Once when we were at Boral visiting our temps, I was approached by a woman who worked in their accounts department. I had seen her before on previous visits and assumed she was a permanent employee. On this occasion she asked if she could transfer to our agency. Her reasoning was that she had temped there for several years and she had never had her agency or consultant contact her during that time for anything other than to chase her time sheet. Through seeing and hearing us call and visit our temps regularly, she saw that she could be part of a team if she worked through us, rather than be the temp her agency forgot!

This was frankly appalling but not at all uncommon. I explained to her that she would first have to contact her agency to resign and ask Boral whether they were okay with her transferring to our payroll. Then, and only then, would I take her on. You must understand that this was very different to a situation in which I approached her and asked her whether she wanted to transfer to our payroll for the same client. That would be considered 'poaching', which is unethical.

On the other hand, we have to accept that temps are free agents just like you, and can choose to work for whoever they choose, which is what happened in this case. We got hours just by displaying our temp care, expertise and professionalism!

Temps are real people who like to know they are valued and not taken for granted. Some recruiters adopt a 'set and forget' attitude to temps. This is a slippery slope that will increase your vulnerability, as clients may hire your temps directly without paying you a temp-to-perm fee. When you look after your temps and care about them, they will be on your side and look after your interests and your livelihood. The clincher in the Boral story was that, when the temp resigned from the other agency and told them why, they had no reply!

I can only hope for their sake and their temps' sake that they have since improved their service.

As a postscript, clients will normally take the side of the temp who wants to transfer, as they value the temp and want to keep them. The client at Boral fully supported the temp's wishes and informed the agency that they wanted to employ the temp through us, as it was the temp's choice in the end.

I believe you need to display your expertise and professionalism at every opportunity as you are in a service business, which is vastly different to selling a physical product. Your reputation is all you have in recruitment and it will precede you, good or bad; guard it, enhance it and build on it.

The point of the Boral example is that the temp could clearly see she was not valued by her employer and our temps were. Some agencies try to have their temps sign an 'exclusive' agreement, where they agree not to work for anyone else. This is, in my opinion, not worth the paper it's written on. Even married people get divorced, so why can't temps leave their agency if they're not happy? How would you feel if you couldn't leave your employer if you were unhappy?

Treat your temps well; value and appreciate them, as they are your employees. The fact that they turn up every day to your client's business makes them your best or worst ambassadors. It's up to you to look after them. If you don't know how, think about what you want from your boss. After having asked this question in many workshops, I know the answers are:

- recognition
- feeling valued
- appreciation
- being rewarded
- being part of the team
- feeling a sense of 'belonging' to you, your agency and to other temps of yours
- being in the loop.

What are you doing to deliver the above benefits to your temps?

In summary:

- Treat your temps with the same dignity and respect with which you would like to be treated.
- Temp loyalty is earned by showing you care about them and their individual preferences.
- Always be ethical; if a temp wants to transfer onto your payroll, ensure it's done correctly so there can be no doubt about who instigated the transfer.

Additional ideas for temp care

How you want to show your appreciation to your temps is up to you and only limited by your imagination. One thing I know for certain is that, the more you do for your temps, the more loyal they will be and the better service you can offer your clients. Here are some ideas for providing temp care:

- Temp of the Month or Temp of the Year Awards (these are also a great marketing tool if you get the clients involved in the nominations; I'll cover this in the next chapter on client service)
- Temp newsletters
- Temp parties – they can be quarterly, semi-annual or annual temp outings such as family picnics or movie nights
- Vouchers or other rewards for referring other temps
- Birthday cards or gifts
- Temp breakfasts or lunches
- Training sessions – these are great because you get to keep your temps' skill sets up-to-date
- Access to discounts, e.g. to coaches, stylists, home loans or gyms (whatever you can negotiate), for being part of your temp team
- Higher pay rate than other agencies
- Loyalty bonuses.

Another thing about benefits for temps is that word spreads. Back in the 1990s at Ecco, our MD decided that we should pay our temps $1 more per hour than other agencies. At first this strategy seemed counter-intuitive as there was high unemployment, which meant that temps were not in a strong position to negotiate a better pay deal. If they didn't want to work at the offered rate, many others would step in instead. However, it became clear that this strategy did pay off. Word got out and soon we were being approached by the best temps. Because we had the highest-quality temps, we could charge the clients premium rates. (It's important that a higher pay rate is borne by the client and not by you, as otherwise it will cut into your hourly margin.) When you treat people well, news travels. When you treat them poorly, the news travels even faster, particularly now in the age of Google reviews and social media. Choose not to look after your temps at your peril!

Lastly, you can spend a lot of time and money on providing various temp benefits, but understand that these are only nice 'extras' to the continuous work you provide them. If you don't provide them with continuous work, all these 'extras' are unlikely to work at all. Temps are just like you and me: they have responsibilities and bills to pay. Finding them work is your number-one priority and if you have this mindset, your desk and hours will flourish.

Chapter 10

Best-practice service for clients

When a client needs a temp, it may be that they need something done quickly, or it may be a longer-term assignment such as maternity leave position or a special project. Regardless of why they need a temp, it's imperative that you provide quality, speed and value in your service delivery.

Being specific and quick will win the assignment nine times out of ten. For me there are some basic but extremely important factors that determine how well you provide the temp service, which ultimately determines how successful you're going to be at building a strong and profitable temp desk.

Provide a service, not a product

You have to consider whether you provide a *service* or a *product* when you supply temps. This is important as you need to be completely clear yourself in order to explain it to the client when and if required. It will be impossible for you to convince your client if you don't have clarity yourself. My strong conviction is that we provide a *service*; it's the work we do around finding the right temp and making the match that the clients pay for. They are not paying for the person, as human beings aren't products that we can just pull off the shelf when we need them. If that were the case, there would be no reason why the client should pay more to one agency than another, as a particular temp may be on both agencies' databases.

Think about when you travel on airlines. A multitude of airlines will get you from A to B, yet we often choose to travel with a more expensive airline due to the service they provide. You may choose not to travel with a low-cost airline because of their poor on-time record, their poor safety record, their narrow seats or their lack of food or luggage allowance (or for all of these reasons at once). It's the same when clients choose which agency they use to hire temps. The deciding factors may be the speedy response time, the ability to secure the same temps again and the comfort of knowing that someone suitable and competent will turn up on the right day. If these and other components of the temp service didn't matter, everyone would be using a budget, no-frills agency. Yet, many clients don't, because they want to deal with an ethical, professional agency that provides top service and people while being knowledgeable about and taking care of all compliance issues so the client company is not at risk. If the latter wasn't a huge factor, more companies would organise their own casuals and temps. However, with all the potential risks involved, it's beneficial for them to outsource this function to an on-hire/temp agency. So, ensure that you or someone in your agency has absolute knowledge of compliance issues or knows how to access the information when required.

Respond quickly

It follows that, if we provide a service, timeliness is important. If you delay getting back to clients with a firm booking, you're not providing them with peace of mind. They may not be able to do their jobs properly as they will be wondering what is happening and even whether they need to give their temp jobs to other agencies, which is detrimental to the client, you and your temps! The client will have to waste more time talking to and dealing with other agencies. You may lose the job and hours. Your temps will lose as you will provide fewer jobs. The speed of response comes down to how effective you have been with your interview process, your availability list and your conveying of the rules and working partnership to your temps. Skimping on the process early on will cost you hours in the long run and, most likely, credibility with temps and clients alike.

If your service doesn't have a set response time (such as 20 minutes) you are not delivering best-practice service. A set response time is also a way of ensuring the client doesn't go elsewhere. If they don't know when you're going to get back to them, and another agency calls them and asks if they have a vacancy, they will most likely say 'yes' as they just want it filled so they can move on with their own job. If, on the other hand, they know you are calling back with a firm booking within 20 minutes, giving someone else the work would unnecessarily complicate the issue.

Be the expert in what you do

If a client places a temp booking with you, you need to advise that you will call them back within your specified timeframe with confirmation of the name of the person you've booked for them. If a client asks to interview the temp or see CVs, they are questioning your expertise! Don't agree to this lightly. If you do, it devalues your expertise and they may be treating you like a low-cost, no-frills, low-expertise recruiter. Once you agree to these terms, you've opened yourself up to time-wasters. After all, if the client thinks they have to do your job for you, as a logical extension of that thought process they also have the right to reject any or all of your temps. The only occasion when I might agree to supplying CVs and interviews for a temp assignment is if it's the first time the client deals with me (as they may have had their fingers burnt in the past from dealing with someone less qualified) *and* it's a long-term assignment such as parental leave or long-service leave. Otherwise, I wish them good luck and ask them to come back if they can't get what they need elsewhere. If a client is worried that the temp might not be up to scratch, refer them to your temp guarantee. If your company doesn't have a temp guarantee, it needs one. If you do the job well, there is virtually no risk in providing a guarantee as you simply won't send someone if you don't think they can do the job. Stand up for your expertise!

Ask questions

Ask as many questions as you need to do your job well. (I'll go through some questions to ask later in the chapter.) Some clients have asked me, the first time I deal with them, if I really need to ask them so many questions. They say that other agencies don't ask that many questions for a temp order. This is my response:

> 'I note that you no longer deal with the other agency, so I gather you weren't completely happy with what you were getting. The reason I ask many questions is to ensure that I know all the specifics, to enable me to get you the best person for the job. Also, the information allows me to properly brief the temp before they arrive so they are confident and happy as well.'

Sometimes recruiters might feel like they are 'bothering' the clients by asking them questions. If you think that, I suggest you examine the reason for this feeling, as it's not a thought that's conducive to becoming a true business partner to your clients. Are you feeling at your core that you are behaving like a salesperson and therefore need to get out of the client's way? Or, do you think you want to be a true consultant and advisor to the client, but your actions state otherwise? It's a privilege for clients to speak with you so you can impart your vast business and recruitment knowledge to them – but only if you believe this yourself. Otherwise, your behaviour will contradict your intentions and clients will immediately pick up on your ambivalence. So, get clear about how you view your role.

This also is about standing up for your expertise. If you truly believe you can add value, don't rush the process of gathering information as this is an opportunity for you to showcase and share your knowledge with your clients. I hear recruiters complain that clients do not value their expertise and won't give them the time of day. The question I have is invariably this: 'Do you value your own expertise, and are you behaving accordingly – are you expecting or even demanding that they give you the time of the day?'

Some recruiters may not like to ask questions as they think they should already know the answers. Well, unless you are a mind-reader, there is no way of knowing how each client does what they do. If you don't ask questions or ask too few, you risk getting it wrong. Again, specificity is gold: it allows you to do your job well and avoid potential conflicts.

A typical chain of client interactions

Keeping the above doctrine in mind, here is a typical series of interactions with a client during a temp vacancy.

1. The client tells you they need a temp

When a client engages you, you take down all the details required for you to have a solid understanding of what they need, who will be looking after the temp, how long the job is for and why they need a temp. The 'why' is crucial as this may open up other opportunities for you to expand your service offering to the client. Maybe they need a temp due to a resignation; then you can ask if you can recruit the perm role for them. Would they consider a temp-to-perm? Is anyone else already recruiting the permanent vacancy for them? This last question is very important as every vacancy has a timeline from when it opens to when it's filled. If you don't ask, you might assume you're at the start of the process, but actually it's been open for a while. By the time you find someone, the client has already filled the vacancy. When this happens, it's not the client's fault, it's yours! You didn't ask or you weren't specific enough with your questions. As mentioned earlier, when something goes wrong, it's usually due to someone not being specific enough. It's up to you to learn, practise and master specificity.

Here are some useful questions to ask to determine where in the recruitment timeline you've come in and whether the client is agreeable to leaving the job with you exclusively:

- 'What is the reason for this vacancy?'
- 'How long has the job been vacant?'
- 'What steps have you taken to date to fill this position?'
- 'Have you listed the position with any other agencies?'

If the position is not listed elsewhere, say the following:

- 'I'm more than happy to work on this position for you. I'm confident we can get a good temp for you. I will pull out all stops to do so. What we find works best is if you can leave the vacancy with us exclusively for 20 minutes. That way you get the best available temp we have, and you can relax and have complete peace of mind that we will fill the job for you. If, for some reason, we can't fill it in 20 minutes, we will let you know as well.'

If the position is already listed elsewhere, ask these questions:

- 'How many agencies are working on it?'
- 'May I ask why the position is still vacant?'

If they are not happy with the temps they've been sent so far, ask these questions:

- 'If you haven't been happy with the temps put forward to you so far, what hasn't been right?'
- 'I can work on it and feel certain that I can fill it for you, but I will need you to give it to me exclusively as my job is also to work on behalf of our temps, and I need to know this is a legitimate job that they can secure when I offer it to them. Can you do that?'

2. You call the client back within the time promised

Once you have all the job details, repeat them back to the client for verification, then tell them you're going to call them back in 20 minutes. Agree on what the current time is first!

When you call back, give them the name of the booked temp and confirm the hourly rate verbally. Then email the client with the rate and ask them to authorise it. If it's the first time you've dealt with them, speak to them about your terms of business (TOBs) and have them sign/agree to them before you start work on filling the job. If you haven't been able to find a temp in the given time, tell the client clearly what you will do – for example, you have two people in mind who are both at work and you won't be able to speak to them until their lunch hour, so, if the client is agreeable, you will call the client back by 1 pm. Always be specific with times and actions so they know exactly what to expect. That way, you are setting the expectation levels, which you can and will meet. If you don't, the client will make up their own expectations and you may disappoint them without even knowing what they were expecting or wanting.

Call back by the agreed time and confirm the booking; or, if you still don't have anyone and you're unsure whether you can fill the job, bite the bullet and tell the client to go elsewhere. While this is not an ideal situation, it is far preferable than leaving the client in the lurch – with no temp and no time for any other recruiters to find someone. To me, that's an absolute no-no. For the record, I have never lost a client by not being able to fill a temp job on a particular day and sending them elsewhere. They would always come back and often comment on how the service and temp they ended up with from another agency weren't very good.

3. Work health and safety check

Ideally, you should conduct a WHS check of the client site where the temp will be working prior to the temp starting. If this is not possible due to time constraints, organise a time to do this with the client, preferably within the first couple of days of the temp starting work. If it is not possible for you to conduct the WHS check due to distance, you can send a checklist to your temp and ask them to fill it out and send you videos and photos of their workplace. The same thing applies if they are working from home. As an employer of on-hire (temp) staff, it is a joint responsibility you have with the host employer (client company) that the workplace is safe. You also need to have an onboarding process for each temp. There are online packages that allow you to do this, which cover other topics apart from physical safety such as bullying, harassment and other psycho-safety hazards in the workplace.

4. First day 15-minute arrival check

On the first day of the assignment, I call 15 minutes after the temp's expected arrival time and speak to the client: 'I'm calling to check that Mary has arrived safely with you?' If the client is busy showing the temp around, the receptionist can often confirm for you whether the temp is there. Tell the client or the receptionist that you will be calling back in three hours to do the three-hour check.

5. First-day quality check

The timing of the first-day quality-check call should be related to your guarantee conditions. We used to offer a four-hour guarantee, which meant that, if the client wasn't satisfied in the first four hours, they would not have to pay for those four hours, plus they would get a replacement temp for free for seven hours. If you do not have a temp guarantee, think about implementing one; in the meantime, do a three-hour check, because most temps need to be paid for a minimum of three hours' work under most awards.

As it's service the client pays for, it's up to you to make that three-hour call rather than wait for them to call you to say the temp isn't working out. It's not that you should expect there to be trouble; on the contrary, it's another opportunity to showcase your commitment to best-practice customer service. Also, in the unlikely event that the temp isn't working out, you don't want to prolong the day as the temp is still entitled to be paid by you.

6. Weekly checks

If the assignment is ongoing, you need to be doing a weekly check with your client. I tell the client upfront that I'll be doing weekly checks to ensure their continued satisfaction with the temp. Occasionally a temp may start to feel so comfortable that they start to take liberties with the client company, such as taking time off or not doing certain tasks. One way of keeping on top of this is to check in on a weekly basis. As your temp is calling you weekly, you can also facilitate any feedback both ways between temp and client. I prefer to speak to the temp first so I can give the client any feedback and also resolve any potential queries for the temp. It doesn't have to be a long call; it's more about providing an open line of communication in case it is needed.

Of course, this is also a good time to ask the client, 'What else can I assist you with for next week?' Every call is a potential business development call if you ask for work. For time-poor recruiters, it's good time management to ask the question while you have your client on the phone. That way you don't have to make separate service calls and business development calls. You can also ask on these weekly service calls, 'Who else hires temps in your company?' or 'Who else might benefit from our services?' Towards the end of the assignment, you can ask the client if the temp is still finishing on the originally booked finish date. If they are uncertain, offer to call them the day before the assignment is due to finish so you know if it's time for you to work on getting the temp their next assignment. I will ask on a Thursday if the temp is still finishing on the Friday. If the client is uncertain, I will tell them that I'll call again on the Friday morning as I don't want to leave the temp stranded and out of work. Sometimes the client will extend the temp rather than risk losing them if there's a possibility they may still be required. If they are finishing up, you can ask the client, after establishing that they were happy with the temp, 'Who else at your company might be able to use Mary's services?' You'll be surprised how helpful clients are when they really like the temp. You're asking them for a referral for Mary rather than for yourself in this instance.

7. On-site visits

It's always advantageous to visit clients in person as they will tell you far more face-to-face than over the phone or on email. If you have temps with a client, you can schedule regular visits depending on the volume of temps used and whether the client's location is convenient to you. Clients may tell you they don't have a need, but when you turn up they are just as likely to give you a vacancy because of the convenience of being able to do it on the spot. The rewards of visiting clients are well worth it for the relationship-building opportunity, and recruitment is relationship-building!

If you ask your clients to nominate for 'Temp of the Month', you can also choose to give the award to a temp they have nominated who is still on site. I call the client and tell them that the nominated temp will be getting the 'Temp of the Month' award for that month and, at a time that suits them, I'd like to come out to do the presentation and take some photos. The prize doesn't have to be extravagant; it might be a double Gold Class movie pass, a $100 gift voucher or a bunch of flowers. What is important is that they receive a certificate for their CV folder and that you make a big deal out of the presentation. With your client's involvement, you will set up both the temp and the client for photos, which you can put into your temp newsletter. It's a double win, as your temp feels valued and appreciated and your client feels listened to as it was their nomination that led to the award. You also have high visibility within the client company to other internal hirers and possibly temps from other agencies who are left wondering why their agency isn't visiting them with gifts and certificates.

Additional ways to add extra service and value to clients

Here are some more ways to add value to the service you offer your clients:

- Offer online time sheets for them to verify rather than them having to print time sheets each week.

- Offer bulk time sheets for multiple temps, so they don't have to verify several individual time sheets but rather can sign off all the temps on the one sheet.

- Offer to go through their on-site WHS induction yourself so you can then conduct the on-site induction for all future temps, meaning they don't have to supply a staff member to do it every single time you have a new temp starting.

- Offer them a 24-hour phone number so they can call you out of hours if they need a temp. That way there won't be any downtime while they wait for your office opening hours. With the client's approval, give your 24-hour number to their receptionist or contact centre manager as well, who can then call you directly if they know they or others can't come to work.

- Offer to benchmark and test the client's staff to identify any internal skills gaps that could be 'plugged' by your temps. This can be done with a number of proprietary tools and charged on a cost-recovery basis or at a markup.

- Offer to manage all the temps – not just from your agency but also temps from other agencies. Many agencies are poor at temp management, and technically it is the client's responsibility. But, if the client agrees, this means all the temps need to go through you for time off, lateness or illness, which means you get to replace the temps who can't work, whether from your agency or not.

- Keep them updated on changes to compliance and legislation – for example, WHS requirements, award increases and workplace conditions.

- Keep them updated on industry-specific news or general business knowledge.

How to take a quality temp job order

Taking a good temp job order means you know exactly what the temp will be doing, who they report to, their standard hours of work, the duration of the assignment, the reason for the vacancy and any other relevant information. When clients ask for a temp, they will often ask for a position title – for example, 'Send me an EA' – but we all know that no two executive assistant jobs are the same.

So, ask questions about the following:

- *Duties:* What does the client want the temp to do? What percentage of the temp's day will be spent doing that? What software will the temp be using? If the client isn't forthcoming or they don't know the answers to your questions, ask if you can speak to the person who is currently in the job.

- *Reporting:* Who will the temp report to (name and title)? Will they work for other people as well? Who has priority? If there are clashing priorities, who will they check with to see what should be done first?

- *Hours and location of work:* For example, will the temp work from 9 am to 5 pm with half an hour for lunch (temps aren't paid for their lunch break)? Ask if there is a set time the temp goes to lunch. If the company has flexi-time, you need to ask if it's better that the temp has set hours to suit the person or people they are going to work for. This is easier for you as the consultant to control. Will the work be conducted in the office, from home or as part of a hybrid model?

- *Duration of the assignment:* You must get clients to be specific about this. Impress upon them how important it is. They may say 'indefinite' or 'ongoing', which may mean three months or six months. You have no idea of what they have in mind. It's not good service to the temp if you can't tell them how long the assignment is for, and it also ends up not being good service to the client. You might say to the temp that the job is for three months, when the client really wants 12 months. After three months the temp may want to leave – this means more work for you as a consultant, as you have to refill the position, and bad service for the client, as they have to retrain someone else. One way of getting clients to be specific is to counter with something outrageous and exaggerated. For example, if they say the job is ongoing, you can ask, 'Will it be for two years then?' The client may then say, 'Oh no, not that long, probably more like four months'. Then you have the information you need. Another scenario is that the client may not want to tell you upfront that the job is for four months because they want to see if they like the temp first. If you suspect this, it's helpful to say, 'If it may be longer-term, it's important you let me know so I can ensure that the person I send you is actually available for the whole duration. As they work as temps, you can finish them up any time; so, if for some reason you no longer need their services, all you need to do is let me know and I'll take care of it for you'.

- *Reason for the vacancy:* Illness, parental leave, long-service leave, project work, resignation: there are many possibilities. The reason they give you can telegraph other opportunities for you, e.g. a perm vacancy, or a long-term contract or temp job. Therefore, it's imperative that you ask the question and wait for the answer. Don't ask and then give them options such as, 'So, what's the reason for this temp vacancy? Is it because of overload?' First of all, it shows a lack of respect for the client if you ask and tell them the answer. Second, you won't find out as much as if you simply wait for the answer. If it is due to a resignation, make sure you ask if they will take a temp-to-perm. Then you can approach your perm candidate base as well as your temps who want a perm job. You will know which of your temp and perm pools to go to.

- *Any other relevant information:* For EAs, for example, do they need to buy personal gifts or do other out-of-the-ordinary things? In one case I know of, an Asian company's CEO had to have a plate with eight biscuits laid out every day as the number eight is lucky and invites prosperity. He rarely ate the eight biscuits, but preparing them was a vital part of the EA's duties. Other duties may include going to the post office to pick up the mail; for this and other errands, ask whether the temp uses their own car and receives a car allowance or if they use a company car. If they use a company car, does that mean the temp must have a full licence for insurance purposes rather than a restricted provisional licence? You can see from the above examples that you need to dig deep into what the temp job is about so that you can tell the temp what they will be doing so they are confident, be confident yourself that you've chosen the best temp for that specific assignment, and offer the client the best service by making the best match in terms of skills, availability and culture fit.

Regarding the example of the EA laying out the biscuits, be aware that not all EAs are willing to do this sort of thing as they may consider it to be beneath them. If you don't know this is a daily duty, you could inadvertently put in a person who refuses to do this and thus causes trouble. Particularly if the temp is to work for the CEO, the consequence may be that you don't even get to replace that temp as the CEO may see you as incompetent! Then you've lost not only the hours but also your professional credibility, which could have been avoided by you asking specific questions. Believe me, the more specific you are at the job-order-taking stage, the easier it is for you to shine and grow your hours. Don't be afraid to ask. If need be, simply explain why you need to know. Remember, this is your area of expertise, so the onus is on you to ask, not on the client to tell you!

Chapter 11

Quality control

Providing an outlet for clients to give you feedback is a must. Any feedback you receive is an opportunity to deepen the relationship you have. You may have had a bad experience with a service provider yourself and decided not to return as a customer. You will probably have told at least one other person about it, so your negative experience has the potential to impact someone else's future buying decision. You may also have posted your decision not to go back via a Google review or similar, which reaches even more people.

If a client loves your service, you'd probably like to know about it as well. With their permission, you may be able to use their positive feedback as a testimonial or LinkedIn recommendation to enhance your sales process.

Either way, you need to create a feedback loop that's easy for clients to use and for you to respond to. If it's negative feedback, respond immediately, because there's nothing worse than taking the time to give feedback and not hearing anything more about it.

I used to own a car made by a French car manufacturer. While I loved this car, I didn't love that it would stall every 8000 kilometres and that I had to be towed each time. Every year this company would ask me for feedback in a satisfaction survey. Twice I described in great detail what seemed to be wrong with the car. No-one ever responded, leaving me frustrated and disappointed. So, only embark on this route of seeking feedback if you are serious and committed to getting that feedback, responding to the client and, preferably, fixing the problem.

You must have a rigorous process in place to back up your commitment to seeking and acting on feedback. Recently a friend of mine bought a phone case from a well-known phone manufacturer. She asked the salesperson for a case that would fit the latest model phone, which her son had purchased. When she brought the case home, it didn't fit. She subsequently complained via an online survey form and promptly received a phone call from their customer service department. Unfortunately, they rang at an inconvenient time. They asked her when they should call back but failed to do so at the nominated time. This company gets brownie points for asking for feedback and then responding to the feedback, but unfortunately doesn't seem to have a process that guarantees the follow-up call happens. For your temp desk, decide what your feedback process is going to be, so your quality control can continuously evolve in line with your own standards and client expectations.

Some recruitment companies have a particular person that looks after this area – for example, a client experience manager. If you don't have the overheads or volume of business to have a dedicated person for this role, that's okay, as long as the feedback request loop begins and ends with someone other than the consultant who does the actual recruiting and liaising with the client. The reason for this is that, while the client may want something in the service delivery to be tweaked, they may really like the consultant and not want to upset the relationship they have with that person. It's better if the client can clearly see that their feedback goes to the general manager or managing director of the agency. It allows them to be open about the service delivery process. I've had instances when clients have loved the service provided but, for example, didn't like the layout of our invoices. As this kind of thing has nothing to do with the temp consultant, it makes sense that there be a different forum for the client to bring this up.

Feedback can be requested via an emailed feedback form generated from an administrator's email address but sent on behalf of the director.

A good feedback form for temps needs to measure client satisfaction in two separate areas:

1. *The quality of the temp:* their skill level, the client's willingness to reemploy the same temp and whether they would nominate this temp for the Temp of the Month award.

2. *The quality of the consultant's service:* response time, how accurately they matched the temp to the client's requirements and whether they would recommend this temp consultant for a Consultant of the Year award (if you have such an award).

Don't make the feedback form too onerous or people won't take the time to complete it. If a form takes more than a few minutes to fill out, it makes me wonder whether the writer could have spent more time working on the quality of their questions to condense them down to exactly what they want to know. Too many questions reveals a lack of clarity on the part of the questioner as to what they consider to be important. At the other end of the spectrum is the use of the Net Promoter Score metric, which asks just one question: 'How likely are you to recommend our company/product/service to your friends and colleagues?' The clients are asked to answer using a scale from one to ten. The score is then used to engage customers in a conversation about why they gave the score they did. So, it's a tool to engage customers that also provides the opportunity to further the discussion and turn their perception around if the score was low.

For you to embed a feedback process for quality control purposes, you need to first get clear on what it is you want to measure, what you're going to do with the information collected and who is going to do it. Feedback is your friend; get it, value it and act on it!

Chapter 12

Eight ways to supercharge your temp hours

There are many, many things you can do to grow your desk. The secret is to do them confidently, competently and, most importantly, consistently. Going back to the airline example, it's no good to deliver sensational service on some flights and not on others. Consistency is almost enough to build a brand on. Have you ever heard people say they like to go to McDonald's because, regardless of where the store is in the world, they know exactly what they're going to get? That brand consistency is in itself worth millions of dollars.

To grow your temp desk, you need to have consistent processes that your clients become familiar with and come to rely on for the smooth running of their businesses. Being known for consistent service quality is better than being so generic that you can't stand out in a crowd. The recruitment market is notoriously crowded due to the low entry barrier. According to recent figures provided by Rod Hore (who has contributed a chapter about business valuations to this book), there are approximately 8000 agencies in Australia and 17,000 in the United States.

Keeping this in mind, here are eight processes you can implement and execute brilliantly to stand out.

1. Marketing the same temps back

Always record a client's satisfaction with each particular temp. For example, if your temp is called Susie, ask if they would have Susie back if there's a requirement in future. Every time Susie is available or due to finish an assignment, you phone all the clients that Susie has worked for and ask them if they need Susie before you book her elsewhere. The conversation may sound like this:

> 'Hi Bob, remember Susie, who worked for you a couple of months ago in accounts? She's just become available and I know how much you liked having her on your team when Janice was away, so I'm calling to give you first dibs on her before I book her elsewhere. She really enjoyed working with you as well. What work might you have that Susie can do?'

If the client is unsure:

> 'As Susie is such a good temp, it's my job to keep her in work and happy, so if you're not sure whether you have something for her then I'll be calling other clients to secure her some work. Would you like me to check back with you later today?'

Have you ever been in a situation where another agency has sent 'your' temp back to 'your' client? It hurts, right? So make sure you are on top of your temps' availabilities at all times. From a service point of view, it's excellent service to both your temp and your client, and it's so easy to do!

2. Becoming an expert in your client's peak periods

Every business, government department or industry has its own peak periods. Providing first-class service means knowing and anticipating what your clients might need and then offering them that requirement *before* they even ask. When you think back to first-class service you've received, aren't you often most impressed when you've been offered something over and above what you expected or before you even thought about it? It's the little things that make all the difference, like having your car washed when it's in for a service: something extra they thought about that makes you feel they care. This is what most people consider to be exceptional service.

When I worked with a few electronics companies, I quickly learnt that their peak period to cope with the increased consumer demand for electronics products at Christmas was all over by the end of September. Their ramp-up period was early as the products had to be ordered, stocked and distributed in the months before Christmas – not weeks or days, when we (the consumers) are thinking about Christmas. This led me to talk to them about their upcoming temp needs in June or July, just as they were about to plan for the busy period. Your aim is to be part of your clients' normal planning and execution process, not an afterthought. This is your way of showing that you understand their challenges and that you care. There is no greater satisfaction than being at the table planning with your clients!

3. Creating opportunities with proactive selling

When I first started in recruitment, I used to phone clients and ask if they needed a temp, which was a hugely ineffective way of servicing clients and growing my desk. As a recruiter, you are the expert in problem-solving and, therefore, you need to know when your clients can use a temp to alleviate a problem.

Here are some examples of situations when a temp can cover for clients:

- holidays
- sick leave
- parental leave
- long-service leave
- carer's leave
- bereavement leave
- domestic violence leave

- seasonal peaks, e.g. Christmas
- industry peaks, e.g. September for the electronics industry
- gaps created by redundancies
- end of financial year, which can be March, June, September or December depending on where the client company is from and where it reports to in the world
- while recruiting for permanent positions to allow enough time to find the right person
- WorkCover return-to-work situations when the returning worker may be on reduced duties or time
- training
- external temp trainers used to upskill internal staff
- company events, e.g. special occasion lunches and product launches
- trade exhibitions and fairs
- relocation
- implementing new systems, e.g. new computer systems
- permanent headcount hiring freezes, when they can only hire temps as they aren't part of 'headcount'
- secondment of staff to other areas of the business
- special projects, e.g. working on tenders or implementing Lean efficiency processes.

This list is just to get you started and is by no means exhaustive. The great thing about building a temp desk is that you are only limited by your imagination. Don't be limited by your clients' imaginations.

Special events create opportunities. For example, during natural disasters such as fires and floods, insurance companies are inundated with customers wanting to lodge claims, so their need for temps skyrockets. If you hear that a bank's computer system has gone down, the same applies. Constantly keep abreast of what's happening in the news. As a consultant, you are a professional and need to have current business and industry knowledge. Keep up with the news in general and the business news in particular.

Peak times also create opportunities. Along with the peak periods specific to your clients and their industries, there are also peak periods that relate to many industries across the board. For example, if it's coming up to financial year end, many companies want to have a major push on debt collections so they have fewer liabilities. Call all your clients and offer them a collections officer. If it's approaching school holidays, ask your clients whether they have employees who are parents going on leave, as they may need temp cover. Call in advance of Melbourne Cup Day and ask if they will be having a function and need phone cover. There are many more opportunities: become the clients' solution provider before they even have a problem. It's even better if you already have a temp in mind and can float that temp while asking them if they have a need. Make it easy for them to buy! Best of all is if you have a temp they've used before and loved who is available to go back to the same company. It saves the company training time, and it's easier for your temps and for you. Being proactive demonstrates to the client that you have their interests in mind.

Using the examples above, you can now have meaningful conversations with your clients about what's going on in their company rather than just asking if they need a temp. Once you know what's going on, you can use your expertise to suggest a temp as a solution to their specific situation.

Having knowledge about when your clients use temps will also allow you to mitigate any 'slow' periods as it is simply not possible that every client is quiet at the same time. Have a yearly planner where you plot your clients' busy periods – this will allow you to be proactive and prepare for their peak periods so you can add real value to them rather than your service being an afterthought.

4. Using every reference check to market temps back

As discussed in chapter 5, at the end of a normal reference check you should always take the opportunity to try to place the temp with that company again. The only deviation from this rule is if the referee doesn't recommend the person you are reference checking or they've already said they wouldn't have them back. Do this thoroughly as you get to display your expertise here through the questions you ask. I have had referees ask if I am always this thorough when reference checking, to which I reply, 'It's my job to be thorough. As employers, we have to be able to use and rely on each other's experiences with any given employee as a means of predicting their future performance'. This is also an organic segue to asking right at the end, 'It would be remiss of me not to ask if you're the person who hires temps in your company?' If they are and they've said they'd be happy to have that temp back, then you say, 'Well, Susie is actually available for work from next Monday and she did express interest in working with you again. Would you like me to book her for you?' If they are not the decision-maker or person who hires, ask for the name of that person. When you phone that person, you now have a 'warm' link: 'Jack in accounts mentioned that you're the person to speak to regarding the hiring of temp staff. Is this a convenient time for us to have a chat about how you go about doing that?'

Some consultants use automated processes for reference checking. These can save you time and effort. In some instances they can even pick up that the referee is the applicant, as they share the same IP address, which is great. However, do not forget that doing your own reference checks can be a way in with a company for you. It also helps you to sell that particular temp to other clients, as you can share insights gleaned from the reference check.

5. Adhering to best-practice service

In chapter 10, I spoke about the necessity of making weekly service calls to your clients when you have temps working with them. The purpose of these calls is to ensure that your client is happy with the work the temp is doing, to facilitate any communication between the temp and client, to check the temp's finishing date (so you don't lose sight and your temp gets booked by another agency) and to ask what else you can help them with. When you call regularly with the same agenda, the client gets used to what you're calling about and will mentally prepare for your questions. Clients have said to me that they knew I'd be asking if anyone else could use the temp, so they'd already made enquiries on my behalf. Training your clients to work for you is great!

6. Asking the 'magical' sales questions

When I was a young rookie recruiter, my manager Nigel Harse (who features in chapter 15) taught me to ask one of the following questions on every call to clients:

- 'Who else might be able to use this temp?' (Asking for a referral for the temp, which clients are happy to give if they are happy with the temp.)
- 'Who else do you know who might be able to use my services?' (Asking for a referral for you, which they are happy to give if your service is good.)
- 'What else can I help you with?'

I call them 'magical' sales questions because they really work. Many consultants ask 'Is there anything else I can help you with?', to which the answer is more often than not 'no'. The intent of this question is clearly to elicit more business, but the problem is that it's a closed question and too narrow. Usually in sales, we ask closed questions when we want to close – to gain commitment or make a sale. Here we first need to uncover any additional needs, so the open magical sales questions will do just that. Then we can close when we know what to sell.

The beauty of the three magical questions is that they are suitably broad. I once asked the second question and the client said, 'I'm pretty sure that no-one else is hiring in our company at the moment, but I had a beer with a mate last Thursday who mentioned that he's hiring an accounts person'. Naturally, I asked for the friend's details so I could call and get the job, which I did. The friend was very responsive and was happy to be offered the help from his friend and myself.

Another time, I asked the third question on a Friday evening of one of my key accounts who I had dealt with for years. He said, 'Well, I do need a permanent staff member, but you only deal with temps'. This wasn't a particularly proud moment for me as I realised I obviously hadn't been reminding him enough of our other services. I immediately said that while I didn't personally look after perm recruitment, I had two excellent perm recruiters in my team whose perm service equalled what he was used to on the temp side. Fortunately, I was able to uncover and secure the permanent job order for our business.

Has it ever happened to you that you deal with a client for temps, but then they give a permanent job order to another agency and you wonder why? Well, clients can get used to you wearing a certain hat, and maybe you weren't disciplined or consistent enough in asking the magical sales questions to uncover any of their other needs.

7. Adhering to a call cycle

A call cycle is a process whereby you ensure that every prospect and client is contacted on a regular basis so they feel you care enough to call them when they don't have any vacancies for you. If you don't have such a process that you follow consistently, you're still working the transactional recruitment model, which clients are increasingly turning away from and some are even quite put off by.

The challenges for most recruiters in having a sales cycle are twofold:

1. *Setting up a meaningful call cycle:* Some people call every client with the same frequency without regard to their actual potential usage. So, the client who uses five temps a week is called with the same regularity as the client who uses one temp every six months. It makes more sense for you and the client to schedule the calls in line with the client's temp usage.

2. *Prioritising the time to follow it:* What tends to happen is that, when a recruiter has lots of jobs to fill, they neglect keeping in touch with clients. Then, when all their jobs are filled or they are short on their KPIs, that's when they get on the phone with desperation in their hearts that leaks into their conversations. Make no mistake: clients can tell when you're desperate, when you're calling in the hope of making a quick sale, when you're really on the phone for yourself rather than for them. It shows in the language you use, in your lack of regard for their needs and probably in your preparation for the call. In addition, you need to be working on a continuous pipeline of job orders, not just seeking them when you run out of jobs, as it's already too late then for the current week, month or maybe even the quarter!

8. Successfully juggling your three critical tasks every day

You may recall from chapter 1 that great temp consultants make sure they do their three critical tasks every day:

1. *Finding quality temps:* sourcing, attracting, securing and retaining great temps with the desired skill sets.
2. *Finding quality jobs for your temps:* contacting clients by phone, in person, via video or via email.
3. *Matching (reactively and proactively) the right temps to the right clients:* regardless of whether that particular client has a job vacancy or not, offering the client someone who you know would suit their business, especially if their skill set is hard to find.

You may regard doing the three critical tasks as a time-management challenge, but consider this: as everyone has exactly the same amount of hours in a day, isn't it interesting how some people seem to get more done? They may be working hard, but then I'm sure you are too. The difference is that successful people ensure they do the important things first. And the three critical tasks aren't just important but *critical* if you want to succeed as a top-tier temp consultant. Think of it as critical task management rather than time management. Thinking about it this way changed the perspective of quite a few of my coaching clients. Sure, you may have some reluctance and therefore put off making client calls, but think of Brian Tracy's book on procrastinating, *Eat that Frog!*, which advises that you tackle the hardest task first so that the rest of the day is easier. Also, every call is more practice. Remember that mastery comes with 10,000 hours of doing the same task. Start now so you can reach mastery sooner.

Even if you only call two clients today, remember how many avenues you have to market your temp services: reference checks and service calls as well as your sales cycle. Think broadly and do everything as an organic whole rather than thinking 'now I must do marketing'. If done correctly, everything you do is marketing to clients or temps.

Chapter 13

Become an expert to add value

Regardless of what type of recruitment you do, you will potentially be working with two levels of branding. At the macro level, the agency you work for (or own) will have a brand that is known for something. It might be known for recruitment process outsourcing (RPO), perm recruitment, headhunting or temp recruitment and management. At the micro level is your personal brand. Let me give you some examples of these two levels:

- *Macro level:* A coaching client of mine in Melbourne specialises in providing receptionists, which may seem like a very narrow niche but, as this is their speciality, they have become extremely good at it. They don't try to be everything to everybody, but they can provide receptionists to any type and size of company.

- *Micro level:* While working at Ecco Personnel, I chose to focus on the awards and industrial relations area to hone my knowledge. I had a natural interest in this topic, but it was both useful and necessary for me to grow temp desks, branches and staff. Because I focused on learning everything I could in this area, I had the information at my fingertips or knew how to access knowledge when required. This led to me becoming known as the 'awards person'. My colleagues would tell their clients that I could help them with any award information they required.

Years ago a CFO client of mine would bounce tricky recruitment-related questions off me. For example, she would ask about unfair dismissal laws and how she needed to go about giving warnings. In these types of conversations, I would always start with a disclaimer and go on to give my opinion: 'I'm not a lawyer, so you should check with your lawyer to be certain. However my understanding is that you can only give a warning about one specific issue at a time. Then you must allow enough time for the employee to demonstrate that they understand and improve before you move on to another specific issue'. The CFO found these conversations helpful as she didn't have anyone she could talk about this within her company, because of the confidential nature of the matter and due to her position in the company. While I offered this advice free of charge, it benefitted me by deepening the relationship I had with her, and it also meant that I was privy to staff movements prior to them occurring.

There's a lot of talk in recruitment about being a trusted advisor, and one way to do this is to build your expertise and offer a consulting advisory service as a value-add to your recruitment service. Occasionally I hear recruiters complain that their clients don't know something they consider to be basic knowledge. My response is, 'Why should your clients know about your area of expertise?' If they did, they wouldn't need you! Your job is to educate them, which also allows you to put on the 'trusted advisor' hat to demonstrate your expertise and professionalism.

Another 'brand' I developed, albeit organically rather than strategically, was becoming known as the electronics expert. By dealing with the two largest electronics companies in the country, I automatically attracted electronics staff and people who had a particular interest in working in the electronics industry, thereby becoming far more valuable to my electronics clients, as well as being attractive to other electronics companies that also became my clients.

This is why I always recommend approaching your clients' competitors. You already have industry knowledge, understand their lingo and most likely have temps with industry experience, which will save your clients time, money and effort when hiring temps from you.

Micro and macro expertise

When thinking about how you can become an 'expert' or known for something, think on both the macro and micro levels.

On the macro or company level, you may not be able to influence a lot, but you could choose to work a niche within a niche – what is known as a vertical market. An example of a vertical market would be financial planners in the finance industry. Recruitment business owners will, in my experience, listen to a sales strategy that will benefit them and the bottom line. For example, your agency may specialise in accounting shared services and you choose to focus on the banking sector or the manufacturing sector. While you could say that accounting shared services are very similar regardless of the type of company, there are still nuances that will make you an 'expert'.

Expertise can be in an array of areas:

- Industry expertise, e.g. electronics.
- Service-specific expertise, e.g. RPO.
- Recruitment expertise, e.g. setting up and running assessment centres. I set up and ran assessment centres for Goodman Fielder's shared services accounts department. This meant that all applicants to this area of Goodman Fielder had to come through us to work there. It also meant that, if I saw someone who I knew would be the right fit for the company, I could usually get them in as a temp until they could attend the next assessment centre, which we only ran approximately every eight weeks depending on need. As I had become an expert in what Goodman Fielder

needed, I could persuade the managers that hiring the person as a temp would 'keep them off the streets' so we didn't risk losing them to another employer.

- Specific temp service expertise, e.g. rostering and managing large temp numbers such as retail, hospitality or blue-collar staff.
- Systems specific expertise, e.g. SAP.
- Your client's specific needs expertise, e.g. I had clients who confided in me about staff who were in critical roles and were likely to call in sick, so I would already have a replacement on standby, and I knew which departments would have the most sick days, so I prearranged for some temps to be trained in their systems ready to be booked. This also meant that it was difficult for other agencies to get their temps in, as the client had trained my temps, so they had 'skin in the game'. It was in their interests to use the temps that they had invested time and money in training.

These ideas and others can work on the company level while there is still plenty of scope for you to develop your own area of expertise and brand. All it takes is imagination or inspiration to decide what you want to specialise in, and then the hard work of acquiring and maintaining that expertise begins.

Chapter 14

Essential temp metrics

There is a Chinese proverb that says, 'Every thousand-mile journey starts with a single step'.

Growing a temp desk is the same; you just need to know what your steps are. For example, if you're running a white-collar temp desk, your ultimate aim in my view is to bill 1000 hours per week (per consultant). This equates to having 30 temps out per week, as the average week worked per temp is approximately 33 hours. This average allows for part-timers and people having time off. If you currently have ten temps out with approximately 330 hours, your goal this week might be to keep the ten temps out and add another two temps.

If I were working with you to grow your desk, I would expect you to know every morning how many temps you have out that day, how many hours you have for that week and how many temp job orders you still need to get for that week (based on your average number of hours worked per temp) to reach your weekly goal. Some recruiters say they don't know what the hours are until they get the time sheets in from their temps, but this is a weak excuse for not being in control of their desk! Imagine if you worked in an office and had people reporting to you. Would you be expected to know who was in and who was away at any given time? Running a temp desk is no different; the expectation I have of you is the same. The big difference is that you have to be on top of your temp and client conversations to know what's happening, as you're working as a remote manager with your workforce spread between different sites and sometimes even different states or countries. As you're not in the same office as your temps, you can't physically see who is in, but you still need to know.

Here are the reasons your temps must call you when they are sick or away: you know what's going on; you can offer your client a replacement for the duration of absence; temps are less likely to take time off if they don't really need to; and you will know exactly how many temps you need to have out each day to reach your weekly hours goal. If you wait for the time sheets to come in, all you can do is establish that you didn't make your target, as the week has already finished. However, if you know where you stand every single day, that means you can make a concerted effort to reach your shortfall every hour of your week. This is the difference between being proactive and reactive. The best and most successful consultants understand that being proactive means ensuring the three critical tasks are done every day regardless of how many emails they might have in their inbox.

Recording your metrics

Here are the figures you need to record for each week and adjust daily as you get more information (for example, people calling in sick or new job orders).

Number of hours

This is the only true measure of your income if you bill by the hour. You could have 100 temps out, but if they only did a three-hour shift each that week, you would bill 300 hours and have done a lot of work for very little return, as each temp has to be booked, rostered and confirmed. If you deal with contractors and bill by the day, change this metric to number of days booked per week.

Number of temps out

Knowing the number of temps you have out is important as you can tell from how much this figure fluctuates daily and weekly whether you have a solid group of long-term temps out or if they are mostly short-term assignments.

Number of clients

If you have temps out with multiple hirers in a company, count them as separate clients. In a company with decentralised temp recruitment, you will be able to determine how may hirers there are, and this will enable you to gauge your coverage, rather than assuming you have all the business.

Also, the number of clients tells you at a glance whether you're putting all your eggs in one basket. A recruitment company once had all their temps with one company that owned a petrol station chain. The relationship was very solid but, through no fault of theirs, the agency lost all their business overnight when the client closed all the stores and moved interstate.

For this reason, you need to have a mix of clients, with no more than 80% of your business coming from 20% of your clients. Having 100% of your temp business with one client is suicide for a temp desk and potentially for the agency! The 80/20 rule also ensures that you have a mix of different-sized clients in your portfolio. If you only deal with small companies, it will take you a lot more work to get to your weekly target. If you only deal with large companies, you may get to your target hours quicker, but you also have a lot more at stake. The safe and sustainable strategy is to have a mix of clients ranging across small, medium and large companies.

Number of job orders taken

Keep a list of all job orders taken that week, updated daily, so that they can be compared with job orders filled.

Number of job orders filled

The number of job orders you have filled is a good measure of how extensive your temp pool is and how well you can 'control' the temps. By 'control' I mean whether you have good enough rapport with your temps to get their commitment quickly, or whether you spend all your time chasing them only for them to say they can't do the assignment for you. If your aim is to provide best-practice service with a 20-minute call-back service, the number of jobs filled per week should equal the number of jobs taken.

Number of advance job orders

Advance job orders are job orders in hand to start after the current week. These are like gold (if filled) as the more advance job orders you get, the better organised you can be with your temp pool. Also, you will know how many hours you've already got in the weeks ahead. This is your temp hours pipeline.

Number of lost job orders

Lost job orders need to be recorded so you can identify why they were lost:

- Was it a non-core-business job you decided to take on but then couldn't fill? For example, you might specialise in office support, but the client asked you to find a mechanic and you readily agreed without thinking the consequences through.
- Do you need to recruit more temps with the skill set that was required for the job?
- Was it a client who was wasting your time? Did you allow this to happen due to not being specific enough with the job order timeline, exclusivity or 'rules'?
- Do you need to get better at negotiation? Did the client force you into a dollars and cents conversation when you should have been having a value conversation?
- Was it lost due to lack of temp control? Did the temp refuse to do this assignment for you?

If you understand the reasons, you can learn from them. In coaching, there is no failure, only feedback. The only 'failure' would be if you didn't learn from the feedback in any given situation. This is how to improve and get closer to mastery.

Number of temps interviewed

Attracting temps to work for you is one of your critical tasks, so this needs to measured. Measure how many people you interview, how many you take onto your books and where they come from (referrals, Seek, LinkedIn, networking and so on). That way, when you need someone with a particular skill set, you can go straight to the source where the best temps with those skills came from last time.

Number of phone calls made to clients

Client phone calls are marketing phone calls and, as they are part of your three critical tasks, they need to happen daily. You can only count these if you ask for work and you speak to decision-makers. If you count all calls, this will make your calls to job orders ratio blow out. For example, you might make 20 marketing calls per week and get five job orders; that gives you a ratio of four calls to one job order, which is excellent. But, if you count all calls, even non-marketing ones, you might not get any job orders with 20 calls, and then the temptation is to think that you need to make more calls, whereas in fact your calls just aren't targeted enough.

Number of client visits

Again, client visits need to be with the decision-makers. It's not a client visit if you drop your business card to the receptionist and ask for the hiring contact's name. As with phone calls, you need to measure only activity with a decision-maker, and you can only count the visit if you proactively ask for business. If you arrive and give your clients some Easter eggs and wish them a happy Easter, that is not a client visit in the real sense as you haven't asked for any job orders.

Number of finishers

It is important to measure the number of finishers because, while you may have 30 people out working this week, if you have 25 people finishing this week you know you will have to work very hard to find 25 job orders for the following week just to maintain the same numbers.

Number of new starters

If you have 25 finishers but 26 new starters for the following week, you are right on track as you've managed to add one extra temp. When you do your weekly projections, you can use this formula:

Hours in hand = All temps continuing in their assignments
– All finishers this week + All new starters next week.

Then you can look at your hours target for that week and work out how many more job orders you need based on your average number of hours worked per temp.

If you measure all the above information on a daily basis each week for a period of 12 weeks, I can tell at a glance where you need strengthening through training or mentoring.

I can see this by working out the following ratios:

Hours to temps = Average hours worked per temp
e.g. 657 hours: 22 temps = 29.86 average hours worked per temp

Temps to clients = Average number of temps working for each client e.g. 22 temps: 5 clients = 4.4 temps per client

Calls to visits = Average number of marketing calls per visit
e.g. 55 calls: 3 visits = 18.33 calls per visit

Calls to job orders = Average number of marketing calls made to get each job order e.g. 55 calls: 4 job orders = 13.75 calls per job order

Visits to job orders = Average number of visits made to get each job order e.g. 3 visits: 4 job orders = 0.75 visits to 1 job order

The example gives us average hours worked per temp of 29.86 – let's call it 30. If your weekly target is to increase your hours by 100 hours, then you can calculate that you need 3.33 job orders per week in addition to those you already have. From your recorded statistics, you will need to make at least 45.78 (13.73 × 3.33) – let's say 46 – calls to get the 3.33 job orders. That means you must make 9.2 calls per day (46 calls: 5 days = 9.2 calls per day). If you don't make this number of calls, you're not going to get the 100 hours you need that week. The only way to be able to decrease the amount of calls you need to make is to get better at making them – that is, improve your call to job order ratio, which can be done through training and practice.

PART TWO

FOR MANAGERS

AND RECRUITMENT

BUSINESS OWNERS

Up till now I've covered the micro detail of how to set up and work on a temp desk from a consultant's viewpoint. In this part of the book, I want to provide a macro view for recruitment business owners. These chapters address what you need to think about in setting up your business; how you grow the business through monitoring and developing your staff's efficiencies; the finance structures you need; and understanding what factors impact on the future value of a recruitment agency – just in case you have visions of selling up for a massive profit and sailing into the sunset!

Without a macro view, consultants starting their own recruitment businesses can end up merely creating a job for themselves rather than a viable business. Of course, there is nothing wrong with that if that is what they want. Clarity is the name of the game.

As always, I believe that you need to get experts in to cover the areas where you lack expertise yourself. So, for this part of the book, I've chosen five experts in their own fields to share their perspectives about what's important.

Chapter 15

Measuring for success

Nigel Harse
Director, Staffing Industry Metrics

Nigel Harse was my MD at Ecco in the 1990s. Undoubtedly, my success in this industry has partly been due to standing on his shoulders. He taught me how to look for markets even when there didn't seem to be any, to respect the full process he described and to measure, measure, measure – as what you measure, you can improve!

Nigel was hugely successful in growing a national recruitment company in a climate when all our competitors were contracting, closing branches and selling off brands under their umbrellas. Nigel's particular skill was his ability to galvanise our team (even during an economic recession) to believe in ourselves and the 'process'. Nigel broke the recruitment process down and measured everyone's input and output, which is what enabled him to grow both his staff and the business. I know from many current recruitment business owners that they dislike the idea of keeping statistics and the culture they believe it brings. However, you will see from my interview with Nigel that it depends on how you use the statistics you collect. Are you using them to look for parts of the process that need improving, or are you using them to hit your staff over the head?

***

Nigel's input is interesting for a couple of reasons.

Firstly, his company Staffing Industry Metrics collates data from 87 recruitment companies across all sectors in Australia and New Zealand on a monthly basis and has done so for the last 19 years. This means that Nigel has up-to-the-minute information on what the top performers are billing as well as the average billers and the low performers. This data is essential if you want to know how you stack up against your peers in the industry. While the names of the companies are kept confidential, participants still get a complete picture of what is possible out there. Nigel says, 'It may be that you are a high performer but you didn't realise it. Or, maybe you think you're a top biller but find that you're actually pretty average compared to what others are billing in the marketplace. There is no point in kidding yourself about your results – if you know what the best are achieving, then you know what to aim for'. As a professional, it's important that you don't work in isolation and that you are aware of where you stand – and, importantly, what you need to do to improve. Imagine if elite athletes operated in a vacuum and refused to measure their performance. They simply wouldn't know the level of performance needed to make the grade, or whether their training was improving their performance or not.

Secondly, Nigel came to Australia from the United Kingdom to establish and build Ecco Personnel and was my boss from 1990 to 1995 (Ecco merged with Adia in 1996). This was during the recession, the one we 'had to have' in Australia, when interest rates peaked at 17.5% and the unemployment rate was close to 11%. Yet, during this time he managed to steer his team, of which I was a very happy member, to growth and profit in a market where many jobs had disappeared. I wanted his view on what has changed in the temp recruitment industry.

Unsurprisingly, Nigel is a big fan of measuring activities, because he believes it's important to know that you are honouring your commitments and doing what you promised your clients. If you don't measure things, how do you find the areas you need to improve?

He makes a clear and eloquent point about the difference between being 'in control' and 'controlling'. Being in control is about doing the right activities and measuring them so you can improve your efficiencies. If you don't know what you're doing, it's like working in the dark. Nigel also believes that, as a manager, you have a duty to grow your people. It's your responsibility to make it clear to them that their challenge in taking on the role is to demonstrate they are as good as you or even better. If you don't measure activities, you either don't care or you are shirking your responsibilities. 'Controlling' is when you measure the activities but then don't use the numbers for anything other than beating people over the head.

Back when Nigel started in recruitment in 1977, he had to report on 20 different numbers every day, which included:

- tomorrow starters
- starters later in the week
- how many temps didn't show up at their assignment
- how many jobs were taken that day
- how many advance orders were taken
- how many current assignments were extended
- how many jobs were filled
- how many jobs were unfilled and lost
- how many new temps were starting work
- how many candidates were interviewed
- how many temps were currently working
- how many reference checks were conducted
- the average value of time sheets
- the average number of hours worked per temp
- the average margin as a percentage of pay, as a markup of pay or as gross profit per hour, which are three ways to look at the same figure.

Essentially, it is all about measuring your process so you can work on the parts that need strengthening.

Once you have mastered the basic process and fine-tuned it, you can then progress to a higher level of problem-solving. An example Nigel shared from blue-collar recruitment was when he approached a large tyre-manufacturing company that had experienced ongoing problems meeting its targets on a particular production line. Nigel asked the company to give him full autonomy in running the production line with the people he saw fit. He staffed the line with temps – lots of mums who worked on a part-time afternoon and evening basis. Within one month they reached the full production quota for the first time. 'This was all about using our skill and knowledge to solve a problem, thus adding real bottom-line benefit and value to the client's business. Sadly, this is a far cry from the approach of many order takers out there who call themselves temp "consultants".

Nigel points out that there is a big difference between the 'order takers' and the good temp consultants who are 'order makers'. Order makers sell people and their skills and concepts, and they make suggestions, which in essence is true consulting.

Here is Nigel's advice for people starting or working on a temp desk:

- Sell what you've got first, i.e. sell the temps you already have, the ones that are available or will be available, otherwise you could be making lots of calls and end up with jobs you can't fill.

- You have to have an inherent desire to keep a growing temp or contractor workforce working. You have to commit to finding ongoing jobs for them. In other words, it's not good enough that you only call them if you have work for them. First and foremost, it is your job to find them ongoing work; you should understand that they are relying on you to keep them busy, so they can pay their bills. If you do keep them busy they will reward you with trust, flexibility and loyalty, which can pay great dividends.

- You have to be prepared to deal with and solve problems that arise from managing people. Problems will arise, and your chance to shine will be through taking prompt affirmative action – you need to grab the bull by the horns! We are problem-solvers.

- You must have a willingness to keep control and stay on top of the process of placing the right people quickly, checking they have settled in, ensuring that all time sheets are processed through the payroll and that people are paid correctly and on time, every time.

- A good temp consultant is someone who can juggle and manage priorities. You have to be able to keep many balls in the air at a time, and there is always much to be done! Do the important things constantly because being successful requires a consistent and balanced approach.

- If you have been gathering and keeping up-to-date with relevant market intelligence on your competitor agencies, who they work with and what they provide, it's much easier to find jobs for your temps. You will have a list of your competitors' clients to speak to. You could have a temp who has previously worked with that company through another provider and be able to offer that temp back to the client. What better way to break the ice!

- To be a successful temp consultant you have to be committed to spending as much time on the phone finding jobs as you do interviewing and finding temps (compared to perm consultants, who spend most of their time finding people).

When I asked Nigel how temp recruitment has changed since the 1990s, he said we have lost an opportunity to build face-to-face relationships with temps and clients by offering them online time sheets and online invoicing. Gone are the days when temps had to either bring in their time sheets or pick up their pay cheques, which meant you got to see or speak with your temps once a week. He says that the 'essence of belonging' for temps is critical; without it we have little loyalty from the temps as they don't feel that we care in the same way. In today's environment we must engineer other ways to build a bond between the temps and the agency. When asked what ideas he might have, Nigel said, 'Perhaps a monthly get-together, which could be in different forms. Maybe you provide them with training, or it may be something social'. He considers this aspect of building and cementing a bond so critical that he would even consider paying them to come in for an hour so the temps don't feel like they're doing it just for the agency. After all, it's a partnership, where the temps agree to work for and be loyal to an agency and the agency commits to and provides continuous work for the temps.

Chapter 16

Personal branding

David Wolstenholme
Founder, BrandMeBetter

Since the first edition of this book was published, many things have changed – one being that reviews of your business and service feature so much more prominently in clients' and temps' buying decisions. After all, with so many agencies proliferating, which do they choose? Many of your prospective clients and temps will look at online reviews and your social media presence in making the decision as to whether to work with you, so how you portray yourself to the world matters. Yes, people want to deal with authentic people – so, when prospective clients look at your 'brand', is what they see the real you? In recruitment, all you have is your reputation, which is closely linked to your brand.

In this chapter, marketing and brand expert David Wolstenholme outlines what your personal brand is, and how you can get clarity on your own personal brand and use it to attract your ideal clients and temps.

***

The obsession with personal branding in all areas of people's lives has taken off phenomenally in the last few years. Social media has played a pivotal role in its explosion. The reality is that 'personal brands' have been around forever. Think of religious leaders, sports stars and politicians – they have a brand, and they use different strategies and techniques to position and promote themselves to attract the people they want to connect with.

'Personal branding' started to gain mainstream attention in business following a 1997 article by Tom Peters in the digital magazine *Fast Company*. It Is believed this was the first time the world really started to take note that all of us have a personal brand.

The article kicked off by saying this: 'Big companies understand the importance of brands. Today, in the Age of the Individual, you have to be your own brand'.

I'm of the opinion that there are few industries that can benefit more from individuals having a memorable and consistent personal brand than recruitment. If I told you that developing your own brand – yes, yours – will make your role inherently easier and will compound your commercial success over time, would I catch your attention?

Good.

People have differing opinions on what a personal brand is and what it isn't. A personal brand is your unique promise of value, your why, values, skills and strengths. It's what others say about you; it's what you're known for; it's the place you hold in people's minds; it's how you make people feel. It's your key differentiators, the problems you solve. It's your tone of voice, your image and the way you communicate.

To help simplify this for recruiters I recommend thinking of it as a blend of your *personality* and *reputation*.

The personal 'branding' part is the practice of marketing your brand to build trust and grow your community. Recruiters should never think of this as a short-term exercise, because it's a never-ending focus on serving the people you want to attract and retain.

It doesn't matter if you're a recruiter with ten days' or ten years' experience – the practice of building your brand is a must.

Without wanting to generalise, it's often the case that more experienced recruiters who have already carved out an industry reputation find it more challenging to make the leap and brand themselves online – they worry more and find the change too daunting – while younger, less-experienced recruiters whose reputations are in their infancy feel like they have nothing to lose and embrace social media, and are keen to test different types of marketing.

Creating your brand

So, where should a recruiter start? I suggest beginning with a few exercises.

First, think of a successful brand, whether it's a company or personal brand – ideally one you have a close affinity with or where you're a loyal customer. Then ask yourself the following questions:

- Why did I buy?
- What was different about them from their competitors?
- What's their story, purpose and mission?
- How strongly do I get a sense of what they value most?

Then think about all the brand touchpoints and how they connected with you – your online and offline experiences and how those impacted your buying decisions.

It's more than likely that they were memorable and consistent, and that the brand showcased an ability to 'know' what you wanted while making you feel special. None of this happened by chance – it was planned.

Next, consider how you want your own brand to have this type of cut-through with the clients and candidates you want to attract.

Remember, it's hard to separate your personal brand from digital and social media. If you approach a candidate about a job for the first time, they'll be cautious and will look you up online. So will a hiring manager who needs to get it right the first time. What does your digital footprint sing to them?

Start by googling yourself. Play around with key words your candidates and clients are likely to use; for example, 'retail recruiter casual work Western Sydney'. What comes up? Don't bother searching beyond page two or three, because your prospective temps and clients won't.

Let's say they find your company website and land on your profile. Does it build trust? Does it sell how you can help them? Or, is it just generic waffle?

Have you planted your brand on review/reputation management recruitment platforms like Sourcr? Do you let others do your talking for you? If so, what are they saying? Is there a consistent message in the feedback?

Look at your LinkedIn profile. In all likelihood it's the first thing that will come up on a Google search of your name. As quickly as you review a CV, John – your prospective client – will do the same. What will he learn? Have you intrigued him enough that he will connect with you, or even make contact at all?

Recruitment is a ridiculously competitive industry – so repeat the exercise with some of your direct competitors. Learn from their digital footprint – even look at overseas consultants. They could be creating content that is influencing your target audience. Leverage this for your own ideas. They may have positioned their brand in a way that you can have a similar approach, or you could take a bolder position to stand out and influence. If they've homed in on candidate experience, maybe you can focus on the 'speed of outcomes' you deliver.

Third, do the thing most recruiters fail to even consider: talk to and interview your clients and candidates about your brand. Let them describe to you what your brand is rather than trying to work things out on your own. It's a damn sight easier. You can make this research process as formal or as informal as you like. Hang on to every word and sentence they use, and look for trends: this will form your messaging. Your interviewees will tell you what they need and want from you and, while you're there, you can find out what type of content would be of value.

Here are some questions you might want to ask:

- How would you describe my personality in three words?
- What problem do I solve and what impact has it had on you (your business and customers)?
- How am I different to my competitors?
- What is the one thing you wouldn't want to change about my service?
- Where do you go to learn online, and what type of content do you enjoy consuming?
- What challenges are you facing in your role?

Recruiters are notoriously busy people with lots of different responsibilities, but getting completely bogged down in marketing and taking your foot off the gas with 'selling' and 'consulting' will lead to challenges. In reality, marketing your personal brand is equally important.

Inward thinking

I can't emphasise enough the power of talking to your clients and candidates about how they can help you define your brand. However, it's important to remember that it's called *personal* branding for a reason. It's imperative that you do some inward thinking on who you are, what you bring to the world, what you care about and where you're going. Start by asking yourself these big-picture questions:

- Why do I do what I do?
- Where do I want to get to?
- What are my highest values?
- What are my biggest strengths?
- What do I want to be known for?

Content, content, content!

Because you're reading this book and have already come so far (well done for that!), I suspect you're either already creating content or you're considering it. It's easy to fall into the trap of brain freeze, or have too many ideas bubbling around your head, and feel unsure about what's going to work. It often ends up dropping into the 'too hard' basket, or with the creation of half-hearted content.

You can solve this by selecting your own 'content pillars'. Content pillars are the big topics your personal brand will talk about. Find the overlap between what you're passionate and knowledgeable about and what your audience cares about. You'll quickly become more creative, organised, consistent and on-brand. Starting off with managing just a few pillars, including sub-pillars, can be beneficial. Remember, your pillars can evolve over time. Here's an example of three content pillars:

1. Diversity hiring
2. Top-performing cultures
3. Corporate social responsibility.

So, what are yours going to be?

Finally, be patient. Branding results don't happen overnight. However, when a prospect talks about your content in a meeting and inbound enquiries start coming your way, the penny drops. Your brand is doing the selling for you, and everything becomes that much easier.

Remember: don't try to do too many different things at once with your personal marketing. Try one thing, do it exceptionally well and then experiment. Get clear about talking about the right type of things in the right places. Nurses don't live on LinkedIn, and very senior engineers don't spend too much of their time on Instagram.

Good luck with it, have fun and enjoy your new status as a very marketable brand.

Chapter 17

The legals: protect your business and add value

Martin Richardson
Founder, Ready Set Recruit Legal

Let's be honest: most recruiters see terms of business (TOBs) as a necessary evil that needs to be overcome to allow them to get on with the actual placing of the temps. It is perceived as a boring topic that is not really related to recruitment. However, it is so critical to get the legals right to protect your business, and to work with peace of mind knowing you are meeting your obligations – which is why I was delighted when Martin Richardson agreed to write a chapter on this topic.

Martin is an expert in legal matters for recruitment agencies, so the insights he shares here are priceless.

***

'If you're in the recruitment game, you're in the legal game.'

Having worked with recruiters since 2011, I am more convinced than ever that if you act on this statement, you will protect and build value in your agency.

The flip side is that avoiding the legal game and not playing to the rules can become costly once you've built something worth losing. If you allow someone else to dictate the rules or don't understand (or, worse, ignore) them, you will eventually face challenges – legal claims, lost margin, personal stress, disgruntled employees, exiting clients and a poor reputation.

This chapter is not about making you a lawyer or telling you to turn your agency upside down because you risk losing everything. Instead, it's an overview of the areas to focus on to ensure longer-term protection from nasty surprises and to create real value in your agency – from challenging some common beliefs to understanding your business model.

How do you experience the legals?

Agencies that are the most successful at creating better legal outcomes and value have aligned their legals with their brand.

They know what they stand for and where they're going, and have invested in embedding the legals into the client experience. They create a different experience for themselves, their employees and their clients. They start from a place of curiosity and empathy, not fear or eye rolls!

In my experience, a common set of beliefs impacts whether an agency (and, by extension, its consultants) struggle or succeed with its legal and business outcomes. Here are those I come across the most.

Belief #1 – 'I'm not an expert'

You're not an expert? Guess what – neither are your clients. Many client objections stem from the fact that the person on the other side has the same belief. 'Everyone has signed it.' 'Take it or leave it.' 'You're too expensive.' These thoughts are often designed to avoid the uncomfortable contract discussions that nearly everyone fears. And, here's a great tip: very few people prepare for a negotiation. They wing it.

You're missing an excellent opportunity to create an outstanding legal experience for your clients if you can't confidently engage with them on legal issues and terms and focus on their pressing business needs.

In large businesses, contracts are often created by a separate legal team that requires other functions – such as procurement – to use them 'as is'. Your counterparts probably don't know what's in their contracts.

Clients often seek to standardise responses to make it easier to compare agencies (hence the price focus).

If you're prepared for a negotiation and know your business drivers and what makes you unique, you can take a leadership role with clients and give them some highly valued wins, and you know what you can give away while protecting your agency.

You don't need to be an expert, and you don't need to price match to win business (which is, effectively, giving clients the message that you're no different to your competitors) – you just need to be prepared.

Belief #2 – 'The client will walk away if I try to negotiate'

Let's turn this one around. What if the client *doesn't* walk away and, in your desperation to win their business, the deal you have struck stinks? You're now stuck with bad business and a client you probably shouldn't be working with.

It's one thing to make informed decisions to accept less-than-optimal business – for example, it could be good for your personal brand to have that client on board, increase your volume in leaner times or give you a foot in the door – but to do so blindly and in hope is a disaster waiting to happen. This is especially the case when this is your standard approach to business and the legals. I see this all the time when agencies sign contracts without reading them. They've negotiated their price down, then they sign a contract full of risk. They might wish later that they had walked away.

Never negotiate a contract in isolation, especially after you have negotiated the 'commercials'. Use the contract to balance your trade-offs and wins, and there's less chance of striking a bad deal.

Belief #3 – 'This is how I've always done it'

I love this quote from Steve Jobs: 'Don't be trapped by dogma – which is living with the results of other people's thinking'.

Change is hard, but the law and how business is done are constantly evolving. If you are still working in the same way that was taught to you, and you've accepted that blindly as the only way to do something, your results are tied to someone else's thinking. When it comes to contracts and law, it pays to challenge old ways.

And, again, many client objections are tied to this belief. If you can recognise it in yourself and your agency, you may quickly discover opportunities to convince prospective clients to change the status quo.

Four compliance areas that you must be across

As has been said countless times in this book, a temp desk fundamentally differs from a perm desk. Nowhere is this more evident than in legal compliance.

A temp is your resource (usually a casual employee) working under a host client's direction, supervision and control. This exposes you to several compliance areas that a perm agency doesn't have to deal with.

Labour-hire licensing

As at the date of publication, Victoria, Queensland, the Australian Capital Territory and South Australia require every temp agency that is placing temps in the state/territory (or, for Victoria-based agencies, even outside Victoria) to hold a labour-hire licence.

Don't get confused thinking that 'labour hire' only applies to blue-collar workers. That's a misconception I often hear (as is the misconception that awards only apply to blue-collar temps).

If you run a staffing agency providing temps to clients, you are a labour-hire provider that requires a license (or licenses).

Heavy penalties apply for operating unlicensed, and heavy penalties also apply to clients that use unlicensed providers.

Employment

Where your temp is your employee, you have obligations as an employer under the *Fair Work Act 2009*. This is your business model and one of the main reasons clients use you – so they don't hold those obligations. Therefore, you must meet all your legal obligations under the National Employment Standards, and you will be the party facing any unfair dismissal and other employment claims, whether initiated by the employee or by the regulator.

How you onboard and offboard your temps should be a critical part of your compliance processes to minimise your risk, but also to improve your temps' experience. Make them want to work with you repeatedly by demonstrating that you take your role as their employer seriously.

Safety

All staffing agencies and host clients have a primary duty of care to ensure workers' health and safety. In addition to casual employees who are on-hired, independent contractors will also be 'workers' to whom your safety obligations extend. This may include 'Pty Ltd' contractors, where they are your subcontractors (and, therefore, also the key person doing the work). You must be clear on to whom and how your safety obligations apply.

An agency can contract out of or transfer its WHS obligations to the host client. You always have a shared responsibility to provide safe, healthy working conditions.

Further, WHS duties are ongoing and must be complied with throughout an assignment.

You should never assume the host is taking care of safety. Consider what 'reasonably practicable' means for your staffing model and the sites at which your temps work.

Insurance

At a minimum, you should hold professional indemnity and public liability insurance that specifically covers your temp agency activities.

You should also ensure you have appropriate workers compensation insurance that covers your temp workers. Each state and territory requires workers compensation in its jurisdiction, and requirements (and who needs to be insured) may differ.

You should also consider cybercrime insurance and other business interruption cover.

I recommend you work with a recruitment insurance expert at all times as, again, recruitment is a unique business model. An expert will know what cover you need. An industry association such as the Recruitment, Consulting & Staffing Association (RCSA) or the Association of Professional Staffing Companies (APSCo) is a great place to start if you need a recommendation.

This is not an area where you want to discover too late that you aren't appropriately insured.

Client terms and your services

A temp agency's service is not what its temps do for a client on a day-to-day basis. An agency matches a temp's skills to a client's brief. The agency doesn't hold itself out as a specialist in those temp skills.

Take a tech agency that supplies a developer – is the agency a specialist IT consultancy signing off on software deliverables? I doubt it.

I see too many contracts (and TOBs) that get this fundamental principle wrong, and leave agencies carrying service delivery risk and becoming their client's default insurer.

What you call the service doesn't matter – temp, labour hire, contract, statement of work or staff augmentation. It only matters where the service delivery risk sits and what liability you sign up for.

When dealing with client contracts:

1. assume the contract is unsuitable for a tri-party staffing model – agency, client, temp
2. remember that what a temp does for your client is not your agency's services

3. your insurer should see a contract before you sign it. If a contract pushes certain risks onto you and you haven't had it ticked off by your insurer, you might be out of luck if a claim occurs

4. temp conversions, fee adjustments, payment terms and risk allocation terms will undoubtedly be missing or much less favourable than your usual terms.

Nailing your temp engagement model

In my experience, unfortunately, many agencies and consultants don't adequately understand the legal engagement they rely on as their business model. In simple terms, the law provides a binary choice – you are either engaging temps as (casual) employees or as independent contractors. The ramifications of this decision (or non-decision) can be profound.

You can only address many of the questions of risk I have outlined in this chapter once you understand your temp engagement model. And, the bigger your temp book gets while these questions remain out there, the more pain you face – especially if:

- you are misclassifying your temps as 'independent contractors' when they are probably employees

- you don't understand your legal obligations to casual employees, such as casual conversion and the right for long-term casuals to access unfair dismissal laws.

Do you on-hire PAYG contractors, ABNs, temps, ACNs or other types of 'contractors'? These are all common labels. Labels can get in the way of the true nature of the staffing model in place.

If you're growing or have ambitions to grow your temp book, sense check your business model with these questions:

- How do you engage your temps – as casual employees or independent contractors?

- Why do you do it this way, and is it suitable for your agency?

- What do you want your engagement strategy to be as you grow?
- Who else is part of your supply chain – do you use a contractor management or payroll company? If so, what do their answers to the first two questions mean for you (because it's still your backside on the line contractually and reputationally, and in other regulated areas like safety and labour-hire licensing)?
- Are you using outdated and borrowed legal documents that no-one questions?

The law and the legals touch on every area of running a temp desk, from negotiating great outcomes with clients to understanding the laws that apply to the lifecycle of a temp worker's engagement.

My intent is to challenge the mindset that, if you and your agency ignore your own interests to win business, you may be ignoring the rules of the game. But, there is more to this than dragging you into a game you don't feel you can win! There is gold in understanding the legals and how they apply to your agency. You will create great foundations, improve your outcomes and provide a better experience for your clients and temps.

Don't think you need to become a lawyer; instead, realise the opportunity to become a leading agency by embracing the legals and making them work for you.

Chapter 18

Recruitment tech to power your temp business

Andrew Rodger
CEO and Founder, recMate

Gone are the days when recruiters would have client files on index cards and physical temp files in filing cabinets. Now we have tech, so much tech, to make life easier – but often tech is not used to its full potential. I see so many companies rush out to buy the latest tech without thinking about how it all fits together.

In this chapter, recruitment tech expert Andrew Rodger shares what you need to think about to avoid ending up with a 'franken stack', and how best to use tech to support your temp desk and business goals.

***

Recruitment technology (rec-tech) can be an amazing asset to make your team more productive, help you deliver best-practice customer service and enable you to scale as you grow.

Over the past five years, rec-tech has become much more available and affordable for all teams. It's become an essential ingredient in the recipe of delivering industry-leading levels of service to clients and temps.

Your rec-tech stack is also becoming a key element in a recruitment professional's decision to join (or leave!) your agency. Most top performers consider the tools available to help make their roles more productive and profitable when assessing which agency to work for, so it's critical that tech is part of your attraction and retention strategy.

It starts with your recruitment database

Your recruitment database – the engine that houses your candidates, clients, jobs and placements and allows you to report on how your business and team members are tracking against targets – is your core piece of rec-tech. When you're considering which database to use, it's important to think about not just your current business requirements but those of your future, too. Will the platform be flexible to scale up or down with you?

Many databases are great for perm recruitment but may not meet your needs as a temp recruiter. You must make sure your database acts as an asset to collect the following information about your candidates and temps:

- *Availability:* a status field that allows you to code whether your temps are available, placed, do not contact or archived.
- *Date availability:* so you can filter candidates available now, next week or next month (whenever the temp role is required).
- *Rates:* it's no good finding the perfect temp if the role is below their pay grade.
- *Placement and assignment history:* an easy way to see where your temps have worked for you before at a glance.
- *Contact details:* mobile number and email are key here. Keeping these up-to-date can be a burden, but automation can assist with this.

- *Notes:* commentary either in a single field or a section to highlight each interaction your business has had with the individual. This should include your interview notes and/or video recording (if you are doing a video interview).
- *Files:* capacity to upload and search for the temp's CV, references, qualifications, visas and other supporting documentation. Many platforms provide the temp with the ability to upload key documents, such as a CV, and leading platforms will highlight when certain documents are about to expire (such as a visa end date) and contact the temp to request upload of an updated version.
- *Skills and experience:* skills and industry experience should be able to be easily 'coded' against the temp. These codes are invaluable to quickly search for temps who meet the job brief.

Recruitment-specific databases will also have the following abilities:

- Storing company and client contact information
- Storing jobs (and accompanying advertisements to push to your website/job boards, with applications coming back into the database against the job)
- Recording placement activity.

Each of these elements should be able to link with one another. ('Relational database' is the tech jargon!) This means that, for example, you should be able to look at a temp's record and see which jobs they have carried out for your clients. This allows you to build key reports that are essential to professionally managing your business (metrics such as time to fill and job to placement).

Managing your temps when they are placed is key to running a lucrative temp desk, so make sure the database can easily track core data points to manage your business, including:

- current temps out
- the duration they will be working (start and end date)
- their margins
- when they are up for extension/termination.

The system should have the ability to house other essential details, such as the hiring manager and time sheet approver's name and contact details, so that this can be used when creating contracts and keeping in contact with key stakeholders when your temp is on site (and when it comes time to extend/complete the placement).

Reviewing all this information manually is impossible, so it's important to ensure your database has strong reporting capabilities.

Reporting

Housing all your recruitment data is one element of the rec-tech ecosystem; reporting on how your business is performing is also essential so that you and your team can make data-driven decisions.

This book has highlighted several key metrics you must manage when running a successful temp business, and your system should produce these. Make sure it can report on:

- client activity (calls/meetings)
- jobs added in period
- job activities:
  - number of applications
  - internal interviews
  - placements
  - billable hours
  - extensions
  - early terminations
- time to fill
- current temps out
- jobs lost (and why – e.g. lost to competitor, withdrawn, filled internally)
- key ratios:
  - client calls/meetings to job orders
  - meetings to job orders
  - job order to placement

Setting targets, goals or KPIs for your individual team members and the business as a whole is important. A platform that can report on this is essential to self-management for team members and your leadership team. Leading platforms will 'gamify' this data in interactive leader boards to highlight success. There's nothing wrong with a bit of positive peer-group pressure!

Recruitment databases hold so much information that can become unwieldy and outdated very quickly. Many platforms now have recruitment automation tools to assist with data management, which can help you deliver first-class customer service to your clients and temps alike.

Recruitment automation

Creating efficiencies in your business is key to scalability. The more time you and your team spend manually maintaining your database and unnecessarily interacting with unplaceable applicants, the less time you have to spend sourcing temps, building client relationships and making placements.

Automation in recruitment allows you to set up routines that translate in your team clawing back time to increase productivity, accelerate time to fill, reduce cost per hire and, ultimately, lead to a more profitable business.

Many recruitment platforms now have modules that allow you to set up recurring journeys your team would normally have to manually perform. Automation can often be used to streamline key areas of recruitment that are core to running a successful business.

Temp sourcing and data hygiene

Automation can be used to identify temps who meet a job brief (based on data held on file) and alert the job owner. It can also be used to contact and screen matched temps to identify who is available and meets the role criteria.

Data hygiene is a key downfall of many agencies. Why not automate this time-consuming process and keep temp engagement levels high at the same time? Automation can be used to contact temps who your business has not been in contact with recently (either because they haven't worked for you or their last job was more than six months ago) to increase engagement and keep key data points (such as their contact information and availability) up-to-date. Many platforms will then update the temp's record with this collected information and can be set up to alert a staff member when this occurs.

Screening job applications and communicating with temps

Sometimes you will have hundreds of applications for jobs you advertise. Using automation to acknowledge receipt and perform some applicant screening is invaluable for delivering best-practice customer service levels and saving your team valuable time. Simple screening questions, such as around desired rates, residency status and availability, can efficiently rule in or out applicants before your team members even see a CV. It's not uncommon to have applicants from across the globe apply for roles, and their visa status may be a hard stop in their progress. Automation can identify this, then automatically reject them via email and, if you desire, archive that applicant's record so your team doesn't have to.

When you have temps in a job cycle – application, shortlist, internal interview, reference checks and so on – automation can keep your candidate up-to-date and confirm key information.

Post-placement care

Keeping in touch with placed temps and their hiring managers is a core requirement of delivering best-practice customer experience. Many agencies promise great things but fail – not for lack of trying but usually because of a lack of time or organisation.

Automation can drive your post-placement care by automatically putting your placed temp into a post-placement care cycle, which could include check points reminding the consultant to perform certain actions throughout the cycle (see chapters 10 and 11 for more information on the recommended actions).

Client management

Keeping in contact with clients is key to ensure you are across their needs and can service them when they need assistance. For example, automation can be set to alert your team members when a client has not been contacted for a certain period of time so they are prompted to make a call.

General marketing

Put your key clients and temps into a general marketing cycle. Having monthly or quarterly mail-shots that include market trends, white papers, blog posts and recent salary/rate survey information is a great way to keep in touch with your key contacts and build your company's brand. It will help keep you top of mind.

Additional rec-tech tools

The world of recruitment tech is growing daily. Here are some of the many elements you can add to your core recruitment database:

- *Sourcing tools:* these efficiently scour the web, including paid candidate databases, and your internal database to find prospective job matches.
- *Assessment tools:* these include profiling tools, technical tests and similar tools to assist with shortlisting processes.
- *Video interviewing platforms:* these can be used for traditional interviews and/or recording candidate profiles.
- *Reference-checking tools:* these can send out reference check forms to referees, then the references are prepared in your desired format and ready to send to the client.
- *Calendar-booking tools:* these make short work of offering your calendar to clients/applicants to book in appointments, and they send confirmation emails and reminders leading up to the event.
- *Survey tools:* these are often included in automation suites to measure customer satisfaction.

- *Onboarding platforms:* these are usually linked to the core database, taking placement data to enable the temp to complete essential legal processes so they're work-ready and billable quickly.
- *Client/temp portals:* secure areas for clients to review the progress of their jobs you are managing, temp portals often offer the ability for them to update their details and manage alerts for jobs posted to your website.

The Talent Tech Labs website includes a great resource that groups recruitment tech by category. Visit talenttechlabs.com.

The rec-tech landscape has developed to enable your business to do more with less – from anywhere. It's becoming key to agency success.

When considering recruitment tech, draft a checklist of the core requirements (like you would a job brief for a client) that your business needs to run successfully.

Your chosen recruitment database service provider should be a true partner that will allow you to focus on the people side of your business rather than spending time and money on inefficient processes. Also, don't forget to do an annual health check of your recruitment tech ecosystem to ensure you are using each piece of technology and it has not become shelf-ware.

Chapter 19

How building a temp desk impacts business evaluation

Rod Hore
Director, HHMC

In this chapter, Rod Hore gives us a valuable insight into what buyers of recruitment businesses look for, and which factors increase the value of the business and which factors don't – even though you might think they should! This chapter is largely extracted from an article previously published on the HHMC website.

Rod, who I know through Nigel Harse, is well connected not just in the Australian market but on a global scale. He can speak knowledgeably about market trends anywhere in the world. Rod is a true professional who has great listening and follow-through skills – both important business skills that I'm constantly surprised (or, should I say, disappointed) more people don't display. He is generous with his knowledge and, if you're thinking of buying or selling a recruitment business, he is who you want to have on your team.

***

Larger businesses – for example, those with an independent board – continually make strategy decisions to protect business sustainability. They will have strategies in place for finance, management, sales, client, geographic coverage, product mix and operations capability – all important aspects of business. An area of great focus is building sustainability into the businesses revenue and profit forecasts. The board and executive are asking: what decisions should the business be taking to protect its future?

The adopted strategies will often forfeit high risk/return options for 'steady' options that will deliver predictable revenue and profit. A business that can predict future revenue and profit will be less subject to catastrophic failure and will be valued higher.

The same philosophy applies within the recruitment industry. It means that if you have a business with a substantial contribution away from transaction revenue, such as provided by temp and contract services and other solutions such as recruitment process outsourcing (RPO), you will have a business with greater sustainability and higher value than a similar sized business with little revenue from such services.

This chapter looks at some of the characteristics of business valuation in the recruitment industry, and the impact temp and contract revenue and solutions revenue has on this business valuation. There is a lot of misunderstanding about business valuations in general, but especially in the value of small to medium recruitment agencies.

Recruitment industry business valuations

Very little of the information published on recruitment agency valuations is applicable to small to medium recruitment agencies. Press releases about large deals, especially if they involve listed companies, are misleading. Articles about deals in other countries can be misleading if applied to your market. Most of what happens in business deals with smaller companies in the recruitment industry is not published as it involves deals between private companies that are kept confidential.

There is also a need to have a precise definition when discussing business sale results. Is it a share sale or an asset sale? Is working capital included or not? Are we discussing a multiple of profit before tax or a multiple of profit after tax?

For consistency, unless otherwise qualified, this chapter will discuss small to medium recruitment agency value as a multiple of normalised profit before tax excluding working capital.

Why sustainability matters

Looking at the past two or three years' financial performance is an important part of understanding a recruitment business's capability and potential. However, past performance is not an appropriate guide to future performance and, hence, not an appropriate guide to business value.

For a services industry such as recruitment, the business value may be thought of as the risk associated with a new owner generating profits in the future. The seller is asking the buyer to pay a multiple of future profits for the business. What generated profits in the past? Are those characteristics available for the new owner in the future? Aspects such as client contracts, business development capability, key staff and market conditions all need to be evaluated by the potential buyer.

For these reasons, calculating the 'average of past three years' profit' is not a relevant valuation method and is usually misleading.

The most important determinant of future revenue and profit is actually the size and quality of the forward revenue, as provided by temp and contract and other solutions.

Any agency that is dominated by perm recruitment, no matter what its size or sector, will struggle to attract buyers and achieve a strong value for its business when compared to agencies that have a strong temp and contract focus.

A great example of this is executive search recruitment businesses. These businesses can be strongly branded, influential, profitable, even fast-growing and large, but their sustainability is usually tied up with the performance of the senior search consultants. These senior resources own the client relationships, generate the job opportunities and are instrumental in the execution of the recruitment process. If they want to exit the business, the value of the business exits as well. The sustainability of an executive search business and its value will be lower than other businesses.

HHMC talks about sustainability a lot. We like the definitions provided by Michael E Gerber in his classic book *The E Myth*, which taught us the difference between creating a job and building a business. Many small business owners work in the business and are unable to lift themselves to work on the business. They have created a job for themselves, often with restrictions on their earning capacity and work-life balance.

Smaller companies, almost by definition, struggle with sustainability – they may have single points of failure, such as being reliant on one person for the majority of business development or billings, or one client for the majority of revenue. Any business that fails the sustainability test will not attract a standard valuation.

One of the very few ways an agency of less than, say, five consultants can attempt to prove sustainability is to run a strong temp and contract book.

It should also be noted that longevity is rewarded. A business that has shown the ability to prosper through changes in business conditions and industry evolution will be rewarded with a lower risk rating when being assessed. Conversely, start-up businesses (say, less than three years) or businesses that have not shown the ability to grow and adapt will be assessed accordingly.

What will a buyer pay for?

There are many passionate agency owners who are justifiably proud of their achievements in market positioning, technology implementation, business processes, candidate databases and social media presence. Some are also proud of their logo, website and even office location and fit-out.

These aspects of a business may add to the desirability of an agency – more potential buyers may be interested in evaluating the business. However, what a buyer will pay for a business will primarily be determined by the justified profit forecast for the immediate future.

Investment decisions need to reflect this reality – all investment decisions should be about growing profit in a sustainable manner.

How much temp and contract is enough?

Not all countries have employment laws that encourage a contingent workforce (including temps and contractors). For example, in the Asia-Pacific region, Staffing Industry Analysts quotes New Zealand's staffing industry size as larger than other developed countries in the region, such as Singapore and Hong Kong, and this is because of New Zealand's large contingent workforce. Within countries, not all sectors sustain the same level of temp and contract recruitment – some specialist sectors are dominated by perm recruitment.

As a business strategy, you need to decide if you want your business to be held hostage to fluctuations in economic conditions that can have such a dramatic negative effect on perm recruitment opportunities. If you are seeking to build a sustainable recruitment business, then you need a strong contribution from temp and contract services or other solutions.

If your business specialises in a sector that does not allow it to get at least 25% of gross profit contribution from temp and contract services, then a short- to medium-term strategy should be to commence a complementary business that allows this contribution to grow. Yes, it is that important to the long-term sustainability and viability of your business.

For most small to medium recruitment businesses, we recommend the contribution to gross profit from temp and contract to be 50% or greater.

Some recruitment sectors, such as IT, are dominated by temp and contract services. In these sectors, the contribution to gross profit from temp and contract services should be at least above 50%, and preferably above 70%.

The larger the business, the greater these targets become. For example, a review of the financials of the largest global recruitment businesses shows that they achieve contribution from temp and contract above 90% – that is what is required to build predictability into businesses of that size.

There are exceptions. There are a few global recruitment companies that have built strong sales 'machines' that can compete and win perm assignments, and have been able to do this successfully across geographies and through varied economic cycles. Similarly, there are a few executive search companies that have built strong, enduring global businesses. However, they are the exception.

Not convinced?

We tend to have short memories when learning the lessons of history. The downturns at the turn of the century and during the GFC provided a number of sobering examples of businesses that had catastrophic failures when their perm-dominated business suffered revenue collapse. And these businesses were not all 'average' companies – some were award-winning leaders in their sector.

Compliance capability

Building a temp and contract business comes with personal and business obligations that go far beyond those of a perm-only recruiter.

Your business needs funding, either from retained cash reserves or from a debt facility. Every time you place a temp or contract person, your business will use cash, and you need the capability and capacity to manage that.

Your business will need to be operationally sound, especially in the complex area of time/bill/pay. Falter just once with payroll and your business reputation will be damaged.

There will be a whole range of compliance obligations that come onto your business because of the employment relationship you have with temps and contractors, and because you are managing other people's money.

This topic of compliance, of being 'appropriately corporate' for the business you are building, could have a chapter of its own. Suffice it to say I am supportive of this book's focus and emphasis. It addresses the real frontline for building a sustainable and valuable business. If your recruitment consultants can propose compliant solutions and negotiate compliant contracts with your clients, the rest of your business can more easily be operated in a legal and efficient manner. The back office cannot make bad contracts compliant or profitable; it is the emphasis on consultant training and development that is the winning strategy.

A summary of business valuation

We have discussed small to medium recruitment agency value as a multiple of normalised profit before tax excluding working capital.

The purchase of business assets for cash is the most common structure used for the purchase of small to medium recruitment agencies.

Normalised profit means making adjustments to the revenue and expenses to reflect the business as if someone else was running it. The major adjustments are usually related to shareholders' expenses (some private expenses may be able to be removed) and adjustments to shareholders' salary packages (they may be paying themselves more or less than market rates).

Net working capital, for this purpose, is most easily described as cash plus debtors less creditors less staff entitlements (such as annual leave).

Deal structure affects business value

If a recruitment agency displays strong corporate characteristics, they may attract the attention of professional investors, such as private equity companies or larger agencies. These corporate characteristics usually include less influence from the founders, multiple share-holders, a strong management team, an independent board, a healthy balance sheet, strong financial facilities, strong geographic and/or sector coverage, revenue sustainability and a strong client mix and size. Owner-operator businesses don't tend to have these characteristics.

Purchasers are looking to reduce any risk to their future profits. Sellers are looking to exit their business with as few risks or time delays as possible. The balance of these two requirements impacts the value of a business and is a unique negotiation for each buyer/seller situation.

At one extreme, if a seller wants to sell a business for 100% cash upfront and leave the business immediately, they will receive less for the business because of the high risk to the purchaser.

However, by assisting the purchaser by participating in the business for a period following the sale and reducing the buyer's risk by accepting part payment upfront and the balance on future performance, they can maximise the amount the purchaser will be prepared to pay.

For owner-operator companies there is no such thing as a standard deal, but with reference to all the above comments the values of small to medium recruitment agencies usually have these characteristics:

- The deal structure usually involves about half being paid upfront and the remainder paid on the future performance of the business over an earn-out period of between six and 24 months.

- The multiple of normalised profit before tax most often falls in the range of 2.5 to 4.0. This has not changed for over 15 years but profitability has certainly varied over this period.

- Those small to medium agencies that are sustainable are usually valued in the 2.5 to 3.0 multiple range. A number of positive characteristics are required to justify a multiple over 3.0. However, many small to medium agencies (maybe as many as 50% of all agencies) fail the sustainability test and are valued at less than a multiple of 2.5.

- Many agencies fall into the 'personal services' category and are not able to have a business valuation applied. In these circumstances, the value of work in progress or the value of the temp book may be the value of the business, or an arrangement can be made to transition employment arrangements to a new company.

Advice for small to medium agency owners

There is no single correct strategy for a recruitment agency owner in terms of growth, size, sector or business mix, but you need to understand the implications of your chosen strategy. Don't drift into a particular business mix; make a conscious decision. For example, if you want to run a small, specialist, perm-dominated business that generates good cash returns, that is a valid strategy, but the equity value of the business will be low and the risk of business failure will be high.

All agency owners should have a wealth creation strategy that is more regular, consistent and sustainable than 'one day, sell my business for a lot of money'. Research such as *The Millionaire Mind* by Thomas J Stanley shows that consistently seeking to reward shareholders, in balance with continued business investment, is the most successful wealth creation strategy for small to medium business owners.

Certainly, one road to equity value is to build a temp desk and make it a meaningful part of your business. You will sleep better and you will create greater wealth.

Chapter 20

Temp desk implementation checklist

Here is a checklist of things you need to establish in order to implement a temp desk within your business. If you already have a temp desk, you can still refer to this list to identify anything you may be lacking.

Setting up the temp desk

☐ Create a list of job categories in your niche.

☐ Become familiar with any applicable awards.

☐ Calculate market hourly rates: determine permanent market salaries and divide by 52 weeks and then by 38 hours (including 25% casual loading); and determine on-costs.

☐ Determine your positioning in market and margins with regard to what competitors pay and charge.

☐ Hire consultants with a growth mindset.

☐ Ensure ongoing quality training of consultants.

Building a temp base

Ensure you have the following in place:

- [ ] A variety of sources of temps: advertising, referrals, payrollers (i.e. temps you are payrolling for a client), current people from perm database, career temps (people who prefer to temp)

- [ ] Forms to be filled out when consultants take a job order

- [ ] Interview forms with the relevant interview questions for temp applicants (incorporated into your permanent interview form or a separate form)

- [ ] A written temp agreement stating terms and including permission for you to contact referees supplied

- [ ] A written client contract stating TOBs, hourly rates and temp-to-perm fees

- [ ] An established set of 'rules' for temps and clients

- [ ] Relevant testing

- [ ] A checklist of required tickets, e.g. forklift licence and white card for the construction industry

- [ ] A checklist of work permits and visas, e.g. permanent resident or student visa

- [ ] Reference check forms (questions are slightly different for temps than for perm candidates)

- [ ] A bank account details form and a superannuation form

- [ ] Time sheets, online or physical

- [ ] An induction process for WHS

- [ ] A temp information database

- [ ] An availability list

Back-office requirements

- [ ] Labour-hire licences (check if needed in your state or territory)
- [ ] Payroll
- [ ] Invoicing
- [ ] Compliance, i.e. superannuation, payroll tax, WorkCover
- [ ] Cashflow
- [ ] Financing/funding
- [ ] Contracts for clients
- [ ] Contracts for temps
- [ ] Terms of business (TOBs)
- [ ] Onboarding of temps including WHS checks
- [ ] *Privacy Act 1988* and data security

Higher-level decisions

- [ ] Temp guarantee: what will it be?
- [ ] Market and niche, e.g. government or health industry. Where do you pitch your service? Who are the main competitors in your niche? What are they offering?
- [ ] Organisational structure, e.g. territorial, vertical markets, specialisations.
- [ ] Staff rewards and incentives.
- [ ] Testing: how will it be conducted – online or in office?

Afterword

When I think back to the very first recruitment company I worked for (which I don't usually mention as the company wasn't very ethical and therefore it was a very short-lived experience), I am thankful that the industry has progressed from those dark days. At my first recruitment job, my employer gave me the classifieds section of *The Sydney Morning Herald* and asked me to call all the job advertisers to see if they would agree to let me recruit for them. At my second recruitment job I was given a copy of the *White Pages* telephone book and asked to make 30 cold calls a day. In some ways it's a miracle that the recruitment industry was able to survive those times as, unsurprisingly, the wider business community had a bad impression of us when practices like those were going on.

Now many recruitment companies know the value of training their consultants and are willing to invest both time and money to ensure that their people have a solid skill base and can portray our industry in a professional light.

My desire to write this how-to book was driven by wanting to make it easier and more profitable for consultants and recruitment business owners working in the industry. Through trial and error, training, study, experience and self evaluation I have learnt many lessons that are passed on here. As I mentioned in some of the examples in the book, some lessons took me many months to learn, as I was figuring them out as I went along.

So, what *are* the secrets to running a lucrative temp desk?

- Have a growth mindset; be willing to learn from any experience.
- Don't label yourself, as it limits your potential, which is truly limitless.
- Be open to learning new skills; then practise, practise, practise so you can reach mastery.
- Be disciplined enough to consistently follow the client and temp best-practice process every day.

Thank you to the experts in each their fields who generously contributed to this edition: Nigel Harse, Martin Richardson, David Wolstenholme, Andrew Rodger and Rod Hore.

If you want to contact any of the contributors in this book or myself to stand on our shoulders, please don't hesitate. It's the thirst to learn more that keeps you one step ahead of your competition. The industry is forever evolving and we need to evolve with it!

Please register on my website **youniquecoaching.com.au** for more articles and resources about recruitment, business development and leadership tools.

Email me – **sophie@youniquecoaching.com.au** – to engage in further conversations about temps or any other recruitment-related matters.

All that remains is for me to give you the very best wishes for your success in the recruitment industry and hope that you will find it as rewarding and fulfilling as I have!

References

Malcolm Gladwell 2008, *Outliers: The Story of Success*, Penguin.

Alen Allday 2022, Australia Industry (ANZSIC) Report N7212, IBISWorld

Carol Dweck 2007, *Mindset: The New Psychology of Success*, Ballantyne Books.

Brian Tracy 2006, *Eat That Frog! 21 Great Ways to Stop Procrastinating and Get More Done in Less Time*, Berrett-Koehler Publishers.

Tom Peters 1997, 'The Brand Called You', Fast Company, fastcompany.com/28905/brand-called-you.

Michael E Gerber 1985, *The E Myth: Why Most Businesses Don't Work and What to Do About It*, Ballinger Pub Co.

Dr Thomas J Stanley 2000, *The Millionaire Mind*, Andrews McMeel Publishing.

Glossary

APSCo – The Association of Professional Staffing Companies, part of a global network dedicated to white-collar professional service recruitment across Australia.

Blue-collar – workers who do labouring, picking and packing, driving forklifts and so on.

Casual – a worker hired directly by a client company on a non-permanent basis. Sometimes blue- and orange-collar temps are referred to as 'casuals' although they are sourced and paid through an agency.

Contingent – a non-permanent workforce or employee, whether their employment status is casual, temp or contractor.

Contractor – a person who works for a company under his or her own company name. Contractors pay their own workers' compensation, superannuation, public liability and professional indemnity insurances. They will have their own Australian Business Number (ABN). Contractors are usually paid by the day rather than by the hour. Hourly rates are governed by awards, while contractor conditions aren't, as they have higher day rates that negate the relevant award, or their higher skill levels simply aren't covered by awards.

Data hygiene – the process of cleaning data to ensure that the data stored is accurate, organised and up-to-date.

Orange-collar – people working in mining or mining-related construction work; the orange comes from the orange high-visibility vests that are worn on site.

On-costs – statutory costs, i.e. superannuation, payroll tax and WorkCover that gets loaded onto the hourly rate (along with the casual loading).

On-hire – a person who is recruited and paid by an agency and then 'hired on' to a client. This term defines the legal relationship between the agency, the on-hired person and the client company in Australia and New Zealand. Recruitment companies that offer temp/contracting/casual staff are also referred to as on-hire recruitment companies.

On-hire company – a recruitment company that on-hires temp staff to client companies; its role being the sourcing and screening of all on-hire staff while also taking care of compliance matters relating to the provision of an on-hire employee.

Labour hire – a general term used to describe the hiring of temps and casuals, usually blue-collar workers.

Perm – short for permanent recruitment, e.g. a perm consultant is a recruiter who recruits permanent staff for clients rather than temps and contractors.

RCSA – Recruitment, Consulting & Staffing Association, the peak body for the recruitment and staffing industry in Australia and New Zealand

Staffing – in Australia this is used as a generic term to describe temp and perm placements, whereas in the United States this term is used predominantly for temps.

Temp – short for a temporary worker paid by an agency to work for a client. Temps are traditionally used in office support roles, however this term can be used for anyone who works on a temporary (i.e. not permanent) basis.

Temp metrics – quantitative measurements used to track performance and to forecast the activity required to reach specified goals, such as increased number of temp hours or profitability.

White-collar – most people working in an office, from office support to skilled staff, e.g. draftspeople. Note that more highly skilled people, such as those at middle and upper management levels, usually prefer to be called contractors.

About the author

Sophie Robertson was born to parents from Shanghai and grew up in Hong Kong, Denmark, Canada and the United States before coming to Australia in 1985. Sophie went to school in Canada, the United States and Denmark, where she also attended the University of Copenhagen. Sophie has lived on four continents and speaks English, Danish and Chinese (Shanghai dialect). In Denmark, Sophie studied Cinema Studies at the University of Copenhagen.

Since coming to Australia, Sophie has graduated from the Institute of Personnel Consultants, now part of the Recruitment, Consulting & Staffing Association (RCSA). Sophie is a current member of the RCSA and holds the designation of Fellow (FRCSA), and is also a member of the Association of Professional Staffing Companies (APSCo).

Sophie spent 18 years in various positions within recruitment companies. A career highlight was when she was promoted from rookie consultant to branch manager of Ecco Personnel (now Adecco) within 12 months, and went on to run the most profitable branch out of 30 branches nationally. Sophie later joined a boutique recruitment firm and held various roles, including General Manager and Business Development Director.

It was in 2004, when she was working as Business Development Director, that Sophie's husband Peter died suddenly of a heart attack when their sons were only eight and four years old. Sophie worked in recruitment for another three years until she had an epiphany in 2007. It was coming up to the Easter long weekend and the consultant looking after a major account was going away. Rather than delegating the service delivery to another consultant, Sophie decided to do it herself. On Easter Saturday, while sitting on her couch with a phone to each ear, Sophie saw and heard herself saying to her son Ruben, 'Please go away. Mum is busy'. At that moment it was clear to Sophie that although she was at home, she wasn't really present. Seeing as the boys now only had one parent, the parent they had needed to be present. So, Sophie resigned from the job she had held for more than nine years.

As the boys were still young, Sophie needed a way to put food on the table, so she enrolled in a coaching course. She then founded Younique Coaching, where she offers training and coaching services to recruiters and recruitment business owners.

Sophie did not foresee that the GFC was right around the corner when starting her business. However, she became the resident expert for an online publication on recruitment matters and wrote 101 articles about recruitment from 2008 to 2011. Her opinions on career coaching have been sought by publications as diverse as *The Sydney Morning Herald, Marie Claire* and *Body and Soul* magazine. She attracted all her coaching clients from that writing.

During a personal tragedy, Sophie somehow found a very specific calling within the recruitment industry. It's a role she continues to thrive in today.

About the contributors

Nigel Harse – Director, Staffing Industry Metrics

Nigel Harse is an experienced recruitment industry specialist, commentator and mentor who has a great passion for assisting firms that strive to achieve superior business results by helping them take the steps needed to go from average to great performance levels.

He commenced his recruitment career in 1977 as a consultant on an industrial temp desk with HMS Recruitment (Hestair PLC) in the UK. In 13 years he gained six promotions and in 1989 was appointed regional director with profit responsibility for a diverse network of recruitment operations (industrial, office support, medical and hospitality) throughout the UK. He was approached by Ecco, the world's second-largest global staffing firm; in late 1990, as the recession started, he moved to Australia to manage two underperforming acquisitions for Ecco.

In five years, he took the company from $7 million to over $75 million in sales through an organically grown national network. He personally recruited and trained every staff member and expanded the operation from nine branches in two states to Australia-wide with 35 branches and more than 150 employees. Under his leadership, the Australian subsidiary was consistently ranked in the top three performing operations of the worldwide Ecco Group, and its reputation throughout the 1990s for being one of the fastest-growing Australian firms was well founded.

During the same period Nigel was instrumental in the creation, development and delivery of training for the special interest groups within the National Association of Personnel Consultants (NAPC, now part of RSCA). He served as a councillor for five years and is a former Victorian vice president of NAPC.

After six years at the helm and achieving and exceeding every objective that had been agreed with Ecco, Nigel decided it was time to move on. Six months later Ecco became Adecco.

Nigel was by invitation appointed a director of the listed firm Catalyst in October 2001 until it was sold to Skilled in 2006; he was also CEO and partner of MDB & Co (accountants and business advisors), and as CEO he established and built MDB Insurance Solutions, which he sold in 2008.

In 2003, in response to ongoing requests from industry owners who wanted to have some way of measuring their results and successes against their peers, he created the Recruitment Industry Benchmark (RIB) Report. In Australia it is the only extensive report on business performance specifically for recruitment agencies, and it's now regarded as the nation's most reliable and well-respected measure of how the general recruitment industry is performing. See more at ribreport.com.au. This report is essential reading for recruitment business owners and managers with a profit and loss responsibility. Nigel is offering a free sample of the RIB report to readers of this book. To obtain this invaluable report, email deb@ribreport.com.au; code: Sophie.

Through his endeavours as a business coach and mentor to a number of recruitment firms throughout Australia and New Zealand, Nigel has become a trusted advisor and proven specialist in recruitment industry business performance and operational benchmarking.

David Wolstenholme – Founder, BrandMeBetter

David's career over the last 20 years has focused on three disciplines: sales, recruitment and marketing. You could say people have always been his business. It was working in marketing that created a paradigm shift in his thinking – selling is far easier when you strategically develop your brand and market it.

This shift triggered David to make the leap to build his own personal brand. He developed his value proposition, wrote engaging content, embraced social selling, defined his highest values and openly lived those values both online and offline.

He attracted bigger and more fulfilling clients, selling became easier, and people started searching for him. This significantly increased company revenues, which kept the people above him very happy.

He felt compelled to assist recruiters with this knowledge. Why? Because he has been there. He knows how challenging the job is and he has gained skills that most recruiters are not harnessing or receiving the right kind of support to attain. For the last five years, David has coached, consulted and trained recruiters across five continents.

Right now, it's still the early adopters like those who are reading this book who are making the change.

Martin Richardson – Founder, Ready Set Recruit Legal

The world of work is changing, and it's time to disrupt the old ways of thinking about recruitment. Those agencies that can forge deeper connections with employees, talent and clients will create a better world of work for everyone.

Martin Richardson created Ready Set Recruit Legal because he wants agencies to create successful businesses that are legally protected. He believes recruiters can lead the discussion on the future ways of working while creating extraordinary careers and businesses.

And, by going beyond thinking of the 'legals' as boring legal documents or something to be feared, an agency can transform its sales culture by knowing its value, negotiating better outcomes and building stronger relationships with clients, talent and staff.

Martin draws on his hands-on industry experience running the Adecco legal team to help agencies across Australia. He has plenty of war stories, and he's seen all the things that (should) keep you up at night. But, he's also delivered real success and results to agencies everywhere because he goes beyond 'magic pills' and generic legal documents and advice to get to what matters to agencies and why.

Engaging Martin will reduce your agency's risk, transform your sales culture and increase your profits.

Andrew Rodger – CEO and Founder, recMate

Your consultants are flat out with job vacancies, interviews, client meetings, reference checking and all the other things that go along with being a recruiter. But, does all that noise result in revenue? Is your recruitment business undertaking the right activities? Are you using systems efficiently? Are your consultants' actions actually driving profitability? Calculating true effort and reward can be near impossible without proper systems and optimised configuration, and if you can't see the truth, you can't grow.

That's where Andrew and the team at recMate can help. Leveraging 25-plus years in the recruitment industry, Andrew implements value-add systems that cut through the noise, empowering you with a big-picture perspective and revealing what's making money and what's not.

Structure, people and technology can come together to enable efficiency. That's Andrew's vision, and it's what he achieves for his clients. He draws on his extensive network of contacts offering software services to the recruitment industry, as well as his marketing experience and MBA and business knowledge, to strengthen your recruitment ecosystem, boost visibility over your finances and help you identify real business drivers. Of course, his love for coffee helps, too.

Andrew runs a TechTalks podcast series in conjunction with the RCSA and has delivered keynotes around the globe talking all things rec-tech.

If you are ready to make your systems your competitive advantage, connect with Andrew.

Rod Hore – Director, HHMC

In 1998 Rod Hore founded HHMC Australia to provide buying and selling advisory services to the recruitment industry. He is responsible for the leadership of the group and for undertaking advisory roles and mergers and acquisitions assignments.

Rod has a special interest in providing a range of advisory services and seminars assisting recruitment organisations to achieve their growth and sustainability objectives. He is an accomplished speaker on issues affecting business owners and a regular contributor to recruitment industry publications and the HHMC social media channels.

Rod has been involved in service industries since 1980, commencing his career in information technology. Prior to founding HHMC, Rod had a 20-year record of leadership with local and global information technology consulting companies, working throughout Australia.

Rod has a business degree in information processing and is a graduate of the Australian Institute of Company Directors (AICD). Through HHMC, Rod is an active supporter of the Asia-Pacific recruitment industry. See hhmc.com.au.